TEACHERS' RESOURCES

Creative Activities for the SCHOOL YEAR

WATERBIRD BOOKS
Columbus, Ohio

President: Vincent F. Douglas
Publisher: Tracey E. Dils
Contributor: Sue O'Connell
Project Editors: Joanna Callihan, Teresa Domnauer
Interior Design and Production: Lithokraft

 **Children's Publishing**

This edition published in the United States of America in 2003 by
Waterbird Books, an imprint of McGraw-Hill Children's Publishing,
A Division of The McGraw-Hill Companies
8787 Orion Place
Columbus, Ohio 43240-4027

www.MHkids.com

Library of Congress Cataloging-in-Publication Data is on file with the publisher.

Printed in the United States of America.

1-57768-598-9

1 2 3 4 5 6 7 8 9 10 PHXBK 09 08 07 06 05 04 03

Table of Contents

Dear Teachers,

Creative Activities for the School Year is a compilation of literature, poetry, and hands-on activities for math, science, and social studies. It also contains creative ideas for a variety of fun holiday and seasonal activities.

If you're a new teacher, this book will be a resource you will use time and time again throughout your teaching career. If you're a seasoned veteran, you will be thrilled to have so many good ideas right at your fingertips in one handy resource.

Creative Activities for the School Year is a top-notch teacher resource that will be invaluable to your classroom. It will provide you with enough new ideas for many years to come. This is one resource you'll want to keep right on your desk so that it is always there when you need a new, quick idea.

Sincerely,

Waterbird Books

September Journal Activities

Trace your hand. On it write: name, age, address, phone number, and birthday.	Write 5 words using the letters in the word SEPTEMBER.	Draw and label what you eat for breakfast.	Write a list of 6 words that describe fall.
If you could have 3 wishes, what would they be?	Draw a clock. Show what time you get up each morning.	Draw 3 pictures with the same beginning sound as your first name.	Write the days of the week. Circle today.
Draw a big cloud. Write your favorite daydream inside.	Draw a picture of today's weather. Write 5 words to describe it.	Write 4 addition problems with the answers of 10.	Draw a picture that shows how you get home from school.
Draw or write about what you want to be when you grow up.	Write about your favorite book and draw its story character.	Draw a beautiful fall tree.	Write the names of 6 people in your class.
Write a story about summer.	Write a poem about fall.	Make a poster about your school.	Write a fall story.

October Journal Activities

Write 5 words from the letters in the word OCTOBER.	List safety rules for Trick-or-Treating.	Use art paper to design a Halloween bookmark.	List the first 10 things Columbus might have seen in America.
Count the vowels and consonants in HALLOWEEN. Add the 2 numbers.	Draw a pumpkin patch with a pumpkin for each year of your age.	Write 4 questions that begin with "WHO."	On art paper design a HAUNTED HOUSE.
Design a fire safety poster.	List 5 ways to help prevent fires.	Use art paper to design a Halloween card.	Draw a picture of your Halloween costume.
Write a spooky ghost story.	Draw and label Christopher Columbus' three ships.	Write a letter to the Great Pumpkin.	Draw a spider with 8 legs. Write a spooky word on each leg.
Write a Halloween poem.	Write 5 words that rhyme with bat. Use them in a "batty" poem.	Write a letter to Christopher Columbus.	Make a recipe for stew.

November Journal Activities

Write a list of 10 special things about November.	Write a list of things you are thankful for.	Draw the Mayflower ship sailing to America.	Write 5 questions that Pilgrims and Indians might have asked each other.
List 5 things the Pilgrims learned from the Indians.	List 10 foods that were eaten at the "first" Thanksgiving.	Write a story: "The Pilgrims landed in America and found. . ."	Finish the sentence: "If I sailed on the Mayflower. . ."
Write a story about life on a turkey ranch.	Use art paper to design a Thanksgiving card.	Draw 10 turkey feathers. Write Thanksgiving words on each feather.	Draw a table set for Thanksgiving dinner.
Write a Thanksgiving poem.	Pretend you are a turkey. Write a letter to the owner of a turkey ranch.	Draw a turkey with 5 + 7 colorful feathers.	Finish the sentence: "Thanksgiving is. . ."
Write 5 words from the letters in the word THANKSGIVING.	Draw a Pilgrim's hat with 5 math problems with answers of 8.	Draw a poster advertising the Mayflower trip.	Make a Thanksgiving bookmark. Read a book about Thanksgiving.

December Journal Activities

Draw a picture of your family on Christmas morning or at a Hanukkah party.	Design a special Christmas tree ornament.	Draw a map for Santa to use on Christmas Eve to get to your house.	List as many words as you can that begin with HO!
Finish this sentence: "Santa asked Rudolph to help because. . ."	Draw a picture that tells about your favorite Christmas or Hanukkah song.	Draw a mantle with a stocking for each person in your family.	Design a Hanukkah card.
Write 10 holiday words. Underline each vowel. Circle each consonant.	List 10 words that describe your favorite holiday activity.	Write a menu for a special holiday dinner.	Draw a picture of a gift you are excited to give.
List 5 ways you can share more this holiday season.	Finish this story: "Once upon a time at the North Pole. . ."	Write about what you want to do over the holiday vacation.	Write a story about spending a holiday season in another country.
List 5 words to describe Santa.	Write 5 words from the letters in the word DECEMBER.	Write a holiday poem.	Write a sentence using each letter in the word DECEMBER to start a word.

January Journal Activities

Write or draw your New Year's resolutions.	Draw a January calendar. Write the numbers 1-31.	Draw 4 snowmen. Make each one different.	Finish this sentence: "My favorite winter activity is. . ."
Write words beginning with each letter in the word JANUARY.	Write 1-31. Circle even numbers. Put a line under odd numbers.	Write 3 facts about Martin Luther King, Jr.	Design a card for New Year's.
Draw 8 mittens. Write a winter word in each one.	Draw 5 animals that live in very cold places.	Draw a large mitten. On the mitten, write 5 math problems with answers of 6.	Write a winter story about a penguin.
Write a story about a snowman that would not melt.	Draw an igloo and Eskimo children.	Write 5 questions you would like to ask a snowman.	Write 5 predictions of events you think will happen in the New Year.
Write the twelve months of the year. Tell which month is your favorite and why.	Make a birthday card for Benjamin Franklin.	Write a poem about snow.	Cut out 3 pictures of winter sports from magazines. Write about the pictures.

February Journal Activities

Write 7 sentences about Abraham Lincoln. Begin each sentence with a letter in the word ABRAHAM.	List 10 things that are red. Draw and color 5 of them.	Trace a penny 10 times. Make up 5 math problems using the 10 pennies.	Finish this sentence: "I cannot tell a lie because...."
List 5 foods that are good for you to eat.	Draw 18 - 9 pink hearts and 15 - 6 red hearts.	Draw a February calendar. Write the numbers 1-28 on the squares.	Write 9 sentences about Valentine's Day. Begin each with a letter in the word VALENTINE.
Write 5 questions you would like to have asked George Washington.	Draw a log cabin. Write a story about what it might have been like to live in a log cabin.	Design a special valentine for someone in your family.	Draw a large red heart. Cut it out. Cut it into puzzle pieces. Let a friend put it together.
Write 5 questions you would like to have asked Abraham Lincoln.	Draw a picture that shows the groundhog seeing his shadow.	Finish this sentence: "February is..." Draw a picture of your sentence.	List 5 ways you can be a better friend this Valentine's Day.
Finish this sentence: "Abe Lincoln was a great President because..."	Write a list of words you can make from the letters in the word VALENTINE.	Write a Valentine's Day poem.	February has 28 days. Write 1-28 backwards. Circle each odd number.

March Journal Activities

Finish this sentence: "When I look at clouds I think of. . ."	Draw a sky with 10 fluffy clouds. Write a spring word in each cloud.	Finish this sentence: "March is. . ." Draw a picture of your sentence.	Complete this story: "I had been searching for a four-leaf clover when I . . ."
Draw 16 - 7 green shamrocks.	Make a list of things that begin to change in the spring.	Write 5 sentences about March. Begin each sentence with a letter in the word MARCH.	Design a St. Patrick's Day card for a friend.
Draw a large shamrock. Make a list of things you think are lucky.	Draw a colorful rainbow with a pot of gold at the end.	Draw a black pot. Put 8 + 5 gold coins in the pot.	March has 31 days. List the months that have 31 days.
Write a paragraph describing a leprechaun. Draw his picture.	Write a list of words made from letters in the word LEPRECHAUN.	Draw the steps in planting a spring garden. Write a sentence about each step.	Write a story about a kite that got away.
Make a list of things in your class that are green.	List the spring months of the year.	Design a kite just for you.	Springtime is a compound word. Make a list of 5 compound words.

April Journal Activities

Write a story about a caterpillar who becomes a butterfly.	Draw 6 beautiful butterflies. Make each a different color and design.	List 10 things a ladybug might crawl on, over, or under.	Write a story about having a green thumb.
Finish this sentence: "If I were a butterfly I would..."	Draw a colorful umbrella with the sum of 8 + 7 colorful raindrops above it.	Use art paper to design a butterfly bookmark.	Draw the difference of 14 - 7 flowers. Draw a bee on 9 - 5 of them.
Draw and label 6 things you would like to plant in a garden.	Draw 5 ladybugs. On each draw this many black spots: (1) 9 - 5 (2) 7 + 4 (3) 13 - 3 (4) 2 + 4 (5) 5 + 8.	Draw 10 Easter eggs. Write an Easter word on each.	Design a package of seeds for your favorite flower.
Write a story about a chocolate bunny who comes to life.	Draw your favorite flower. Write a poem about it.	Write 6 sentences about spring. Begin each sentence with a letter in the word SPRING.	Write a list of 10 special things about April.
Write a story about a bear that just woke up from its winter sleep.	Write 5 sentences that tell what a buzzing bee could be saying.	Write and illustrate a spring poem.	Draw a beautiful Easter basket. Fill it with the same number of colored eggs as your age.

May/June Journal Activities

Write a letter to the person who might use your desk next year. Tell them about your year in class.	Finish these sentences: "May is. . ." "June is. . ."	Plan a summer scavenger hunt. Make a list of things to find.	Use art paper to design a flower bookmark.
Write about what you would like to do in the summer.	Write a poem about your favorite summer sport.	Draw a beach scene. Write a story that goes with it.	Design a vacation postcard. Write a message to a friend.
Draw 6 baseballs. In each, write a word from the letters in the word BASEBALL.	Draw a May basket. Fill it with flowers: 9 - 5 red, 2 + 1 purple, 11 - 7 yellow, 11 + 4 orange.	Draw 3 + 6 pink seashells. Write a summer word in each.	List 8 things to pack for a trip. Write them again in ABC order.
Design a sandcastle. Write the directions for building it.	List 5 things that are easier to do in June than in December.	Design a Mother's Day or Father's Day card.	Write a thank-you note to a person who has made this year special.
Finish this sentence: "This year was. . ."	Write 6 sentences about your mother. Begin each with a letter in the word MOTHER.	Write a poem about a hot dog.	List 5 summer safety tips.

September Journal Activities

1. Make a prediction about today.
2. Write a poem about September.
3. Make a list of fall words.
4. Write the names of your state, its capital, and your town. Tell something about your town.
5. Make a list of resolutions you are going to try and keep this school year.
6. List the names of boys and girls in your class alphabetically.
7. Write as many words as you can using only the letters in SEPTEMBER.
8. Write the names of 5 trees and draw a picture of their leaves.
9. Write 10 September nouns. Write an adjective that describes each one.
10. List things that you can see in your classroom that end in "t."
11. Write a math word problem about buying school supplies.
12. Imagine visiting a school in a different country. Write about your first day.
13. Read a book about fall. Write the title and a short summary about the book.
14. Listen! Write all the September sounds you hear in a 10 minute period.
15. Find and write the word "hello" in 4 different languages.
16. Write a sentence in which most of the words begin with an "s."
17. Write the funniest thing that ever happened to you.
18. Describe how to get to school from your house. Draw a map that shows how to get back and forth from school.
19. List 3 traits you think are important in a good teacher.
20. Describe ways to be kind to people.

October Journal Activities

1. Write a spooky story.
2. Write 10 pairs of antonyms.
3. Write an October poem.
4. Make a Halloween card.
5. Design a costume.
6. Write 10 pairs of homonyms.
7. Write a recipe for Halloween soup.
8. Write the names of the countries that border the United States. Write a fact about each country.
9. List safety rules for trick or treating.
10. Write the names of the teams in the World Series. Name a fact about each of their home states.
11. Write a sentence in which most words begin with "o."
12. Write as many words as you can using only the letters in HAUNTED HOUSE.
13. Write a math word problem whose answer is the same as today's date.
14. Design a page for a catalog that sells funny masks.
15. Cut out a ghost. Outline it in black. List Halloween words inside of it.
16. Write what you would tell the men in your crew if you were Christopher Columbus and they were angry at you.
17. List as many words as you can that remind you of October.
18. Write the names of five people who have lived in the White House. Write 2 facts about each person.
19. Pretend you stowed away on Columbus' ship, the Santa Maria. Write a story about what happened when they found you!
20. Write a math word problem using the number of days in October.

November Journal Activities

1. Write a Thanksgiving story.
2. Make a Thanksgiving card.
3. Write 3 things you are thankful for.
4. Write a recipe for your favorite sandwich.
5. Make a placemat for your Thanksgiving dinner.
6. Predict the outcome of the election in your area this month. Tell why you thought this way.
7. Write a story about what a turkey must be thinking on Thanksgiving.
8. Write a list of November words. Include at least 10 words.
9. Use the list of November words you wrote to write a poem about November.
10. Write 3 suggestions about things you would like to see happen or done this year.
11. Using a Venn diagram, compare November to a different month of your choice.
12. Find out Samuel Longhorne Clemens' pen name. Read something he wrote.
13. Write at least 6 adjectives that begin with "n." Write them in alphabetical order.
14. Write what John Philip Sousa and Scott Joplin had in common.
15. Write as many words as you can using only the letters in VETERANS DAY.
16. Look up the word *armistice*. Write its definition and use it in a sentence.
17. Write a poem about Thanksgiving using 3 facts.
18. Design a poster for American Education Week.
19. Write about what the trees in your area look like.
20. Finish this sentence: "I am thankful for. . ."

December Journal Activities

1. Make a Hanukkah card.
2. Write a holiday poem.
3. Design a gingerbread house.
4. Make a Christmas card.
5. List 3 wishes you have for someone else.
6. Write as many words as you can using the letters in HOLIDAY TIME.
7. Write *Happy Holidays* in 2 other languages.
8. Write about a scientist (past or present) who you think is deserving of the Nobel Prize.
9. Write 8 words that rhyme with *sleigh.* Write a poem using at least 4 of them.
10. Write about the preparations that are happening in your home for the holidays.
11. Cut out a candy cane or other holiday item. Write words on it that describe it.
12. Write a story about spending Christmas in another country.
13. Make a crossword puzzle using the words of the season.
14. Write about how you would spend Christmas Eve if you were an elf.
15. List 4 things you could do to bring cheer into the lives of others less fortunate than you.
16. List as many words as you can that begin with HO!
17. Draw and write about your favorite holiday dessert.
18. Write 3 ways you would keep "Peace on Earth."
19. Find out what Halcyon Days are. Write about them.
20. Write 12 words that describe this time of year.

January Journal Activities

1. Write a poem about winter.
2. Write about a January day in Australia.
3. Draw a picture honoring Martin Luther King, Jr.
4. Create a crossword puzzle about January.
5. Write a story about animals in the winter.
6. Write the months of the year in order. Write the number of days in each after its name.
7. Write a math word problem whose answer equals the number of days in January.
8. List your New Year's Resolutions. Record how well you keep them for the month.
9. Write an acrostic poem using the letters in JANUARY. Use words that tell about the month.
10. Create a secret code. Write a sentence that describes winter using this code.
11. Write the name of a city for each letter in WINTER. Write the name of each city's state after it.
12. Write a division math word problem whose answer equals today's date.
13. Write a winter song to the tune of "Twinkle, Twinkle, Little Star."
14. Write 5 words that spell new words when their letters are reversed, such as *net* and *ten*.
15. Write 5 two-word sentences about winter made up of a noun and a verb. Example: *Temperatures fall.*
16. Write a winter tongue twister using words that begin with the letter "s."
17. Write a weather report for the day after tomorrow.
18. Look for animal tracks. Draw and label them.
19. Write a story from a snowman's point of view.
20. Write a story about a bear that decides not to hibernate.

February Journal Activities

1. List 10 bones in your body.
2. Make a valentine for a friend.
3. Write a recipe for cherry pie.
4. Write 20 kind or caring words.
5. Write 10 adjectives that describe George Washington.
6. Write 10 adjectives that describe Abraham Lincoln.
7. Write as many words as you can using only the letters in FEBRUARY.
8. Write the names of your 5 favorite books.
9. List as many of Thomas Edison's inventions as you can.
10. Write as many words as you can using only the letters in VALENTINE.
11. Write 2 of Martin Luther King, Jr.'s quotes and tell what they mean.
12. Write 10 words that remind you of February.
13. Pretend George Washington is coming to visit your class. Write how you would introduce him.
14. Write a story about a mysterious valentine.
15. Make a valentine for a community and/or school helper.
16. Make a seek and find puzzle of February words.
17. Write the first sentence of the Gettysburg Address.
18. Write the names of 5 of your body's organs.
19. Write 5 facts about the Washington Monument.
20. Write about ways to take good care of your heart.

March Journal Activities

1. Design a kite.
2. Name 5 cities in Ireland.
3. Write a "windy" poem.
4. Make a list of green things.
5. Write a spring story.
6. Make a St. Patrick's Day card for a friend.
7. Write at least 10 words made from the letters in SHAMROCK.
8. Write 5 sentences about March. Each sentence should begin with a letter in MARCH.
9. Name 5 women who have made a positive difference in the world.
10. Describe the difference between these greens: emerald, chartreuse, kelly, and teal.
11. List 3 ways life would be different if the telephone had not been invented.
12. Figure out how many minutes you will be in the classroom today.
13. Use the word *green* in 3 different sentences to show how it has different meanings.
14. Write 6 sentences about spring, beginning each with a letter in SPRING.
15. Wind (like wind chimes) and wind (like to wind your clock) are homographs. List 5 more pairs of homographs.
16. Write a story about luck—good or bad.
17. Find and write 3 facts about the planet Uranus.
18. Write a story about a leprechaun.
19. Describe your favorite green foods.
20. Write an acrostic poem for March.

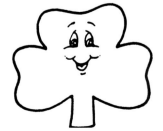

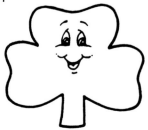

April Journal Activities

1. Write an acrostic poem about April.
2. Write a "muddy" story.
3. Make a list of 20 April words.
4. Design a poster for Earth Day.
5. Write a baseball story.
6. Write a paragraph. Include these words: happy, colorful, and warm.
7. Write 5 things that will improve Earth's environment.
8. Write a paragraph that begins, "The thing that tells me spring is here. . ."
9. Find out from an adult about something silly he or she did as a child. Write about it.
10. Write a story from a worm's point of view.
11. Write a story about a funny April Fool's Day.
12. Make a list of what the government does with the income taxes it receives.
13. Write an April math word problem. Give it to a friend to solve.
14. Write a paragraph that begins, "When my clock springs forward. . ."
15. Write the names of some spring flowers. Draw a garden full of them.
16. Write 5 sentences about how to stay healthy.
17. Write about how things change outdoors in the spring.
18. Write a riddle or joke on an index card.
19. Make an April holiday greeting card.
20. Make a birthday card for a friend with an April birthday.

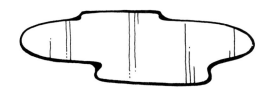

May/June Journal Activities

1. Draw a sunset with crayons on a 9" x 12" piece of paper. On it, write a 2-line poem about a sunset.
2. Plan a picnic. Include time, date, place, and menu.
3. Design a certificate for outstanding progress or an accomplishment.
4. Cut a piece of paper 1 1/2" x 6". Draw something that flies on one end. Use it as a bookmark. Write a description of your drawing on the other end.
5. Write about your favorite day or event of the school year.
6. Write the number of days that are left in this year.
7. Write a poem about the U.S. flag.
8. Make a list of at least 3 of your accomplishments this year.
9. Write a biography about someone famous born this month.
10. Write something you are going to do on summer vacation.
11. Make a card for Mother's Day or Father's Day.
12. Write 5 ways that you can have a safe summer.
13. Write about what you will do on the first day of summer vacation.
14. Write this month's name vertically. After each letter, write 5 adjectives that begin with that letter.
15. Pretend to pack your suitcase. Write what you would take for a week at the lake or in the mountains.
16. Write a patriotic poem honoring May's patriotic holiday.
17. Draw a flower with 8 petals. Write an adjective on each petal that describes today.
18. Figure out how many minutes you were not in school yesterday.
19. Write a poem about what it feels like to be in the water.
20. Write about your favorite sport this time of the year.

Literature Ideas

Silent Reading Club

Set aside time each day for silent reading or quietly looking at books. Make available several books that follow a basic theme or genre. Offer a small reward after reading a certain number of books in that group. Invite students to share a favorite book to stimulate interest in a particular title.

Post favorite books on a bulletin board called, "The Readers' Tree." Create a large tree outline and attach it to a bulletin board or wall. Have students write the titles and authors of their favorite books on leaf cutouts. Have students add their leaves to the tree. Use this to keep track of how many books students read. Students may also use the bulletin board as a resource for choosing books to read.

September Book Selections

✓ Allard, Harry. *Miss Nelson Is Missing.* Boston: Houghton Mifflin, 1977.

This classic book is a great way to open a discussion on classroom rules. How did the students behave when Miss Nelson was their teacher in the beginning of the book? How did they behave when Viola Swamp was their teacher? What did they learn about behavior? What kinds of rules need to be in place so that everyone in your classroom can learn?

✓ Gibbons, Gail. *The Seasons of Arnold's Apple Tree.* San Diego: Harcourt Brace Jovanovich, 1984.

This book shows the growth and changes of an apple tree throughout the year. It also includes a recipe for apple pie and shows a diagram of how an apple cider press works.

✓ London, Jonathan. *Froggy Goes to School.* New York: Penguin Putnam Group, 1996.

Nervous Froggy has a bad dream about the first day of school. When he arrives at school for real, he has more fun than he dreamed! Discuss with students how they felt the night before the first day of school.

✓ Slawson, Michele Benoit. *Apple Picking Time.* New York: Crown, 1994.

This book follows the work of a migrant family as they harvest apples. It includes two pages of apple activities to use as a follow up. Bring in apples and/or cider for the students to snack on while you read.

✓ Thaler, Mike. *The Teacher from the Black Lagoon.* New York: Scholastic, 1989.

This is another great book to read on the first day of school. Discuss what students' expectations were before they met their teacher. What kinds of things did they imagine their teacher would do the first day? What did they think he or she would look like? Have students draw pictures or write about some of their expectations for this school year.

October Book Selections

✓ Gackenbach, Dick. *Harry and the Terrible Whatzit*. New York: Seabury Press, 1977.

This story is about a boy who imagines a whatzit is living in his basement. A great follow-up activity is to have students draw and/or write about what they think is really in Harry's basement. Glue half a sheet of lined paper to the bottom of plain white drawing paper. Then take a tan or brown sheet of paper, cut, and glue it to look like an opening door. Students then draw their version of the whatzit inside the door flap. They write about what happened to Harry on the lined paper. When finished, put the pages together to make a class book entitled, "What Did Harry's Whatzit Look Like?"

As an extension, have students use the same idea to write about something of which they are afraid. This could be a monster under the bed, lightning, dogs, or the dark. Have students use the door to draw a picture of their fear. Share these writings as a class.

✓ Winters, Kay. *The Teeny Tiny Ghost*. New York: HarperCollins Publishers, 1997.

This story is about a tiny ghost who is afraid of Halloween and of scaring people. It is written in a pattern that is easy to imitate in a follow-up writing activity. Students write and illustrate their own versions of the pattern the story follows, such as "The teeny tiny _____ and his teeny tiny _____ went to a teeny tiny _____." (Younger students may dictate their ideas to an older learning buddy or adult helper.) Put the student pages together in a class book entitled, "Our Teeny Tiny Stories."

✓ Titherington, Jeanne. *Pumpkin Pumpkin*. New York: Mulberry Books, 1986.

This story contains a very simple explanation of the growth process of a pumpkin. Read the story to younger students. Then have each student plant a pumpkinseed in a foam cup and place it in a well-lit window. Students then write their own pumpkin-planting stories.

✓ Gibbons, Gail. *The Pumpkin Book.* New York: Holiday House, 1999.

This book shows how a pumpkin grows from a seed. Here are some possible follow-up activities.

 Make pumpkin muffins or bread.

 Carve a class pumpkin. Save the seeds and bake them for a snack. Separate seeds from the pulp, place seeds on a greased pan, sprinkle with salt, then bake at 350° F (180° C) until lightly browned.

 Place an egg carton and a container of dried pumpkinseeds in a math center. Write twelve math problems on small pieces of paper. Place one in each egg section. Students place the correct number of seeds in the sections to answer the problems.

Other pumpkin stories include:

✓ Rockwell, Anne. *Apples and Pumpkins.* New York: Macmillan Publishing Company, 1989.

✓ Rockwell, Anne. *Pumpkin Day, Pumpkin Night.* New York: Walker and Company, 1999.

✓ White, Linda. *Too Many Pumpkins.* New York: Holiday House, 1996.

✓ Maestro, Betsy. *Why Do Leaves Change Color?* New York: HarperCollins, 1994.

In this book, learn about different kinds of leaves and how they change color. Go on your own leaf-collecting expedition to a nearby park. There are instructions in the back of Maestro's book for doing leaf rubbings and for pressing leaves between wax paper. Both make great art projects.

✓ Robbins, Ken. *Autumn Leaves.* New York: Scholastic Press, 1998.

This book contains more details about leaves and includes beautiful photographs of different leaves and trees. Have students collect leaves to label and share with the class. Leaves are also wonderful for making prints on paper or cloth. Lightly paint the veiny side of the leaf with a brush, flip over, and press onto paper. For less mess, carefully place a sheet of paper over the painted leaves and then press.

November Book Selections

✓ Brown, Marc. *Arthur's Thanksgiving.* Boston: Little, Brown, and Company, 1983.

Arthur the aardvark directs his class's Thanksgiving play and leads a hunt for the perfect Thanksgiving turkey. Use this as a lead-in for your own class play. Choose parts and use the dialogue from the book.

✓ Child, Lydia Maria. *Over the River and Through the Wood.* New York: Coward, McCann & Geoghegan, 1974.

This humorous book takes the traditional words from the song and modifies them for modern day. Compare this version with more traditional versions of the song. Have students draw personal pictures to go with the traditional words. Have them describe how they travel to a grandparent's or a relative's home for the holidays.

✓ Devlin, Wende and Harry. *Cranberry Thanksgiving.* New York: Aladdin Books, 1990.

This story is about a family that invites someone new to their Thanksgiving dinner each year. Have students brainstorm whom they would invite to their Thanksgiving dinner if they could invite anyone they wanted. Have students polish and illustrate stories about their special dinners. Bind in a classroom book. *Cranberry Thanksgiving* also includes a recipe for cranberry bread that you may want to make as a class.

✓ George, Jean Craighead. *The First Thanksgiving.* New York: Philomel Books, 1993.

This book gives more detail about the first Thanksgiving through text and pictures that are appropriate for older children. Have students choose one element from the story and elaborate by writing their own story, possibly using other resources.

✓ Nielsen, Shelly. *Celebrating Thanksgiving.* Edina, MN: Abdo & Daughters, 1992.

Highlights of the holiday are introduced using rhyming text. This would also be a good book to use for choral readings.

✓ Ross, Katharine. *The Story of the Pilgrims.* New York: Random House, 1995.

This book helps younger children understand what it was like being a Pilgrim. It uses simple text and pictures. Read the book and discuss how students might have been able to help out in such needy times. Bring in old shoeboxes and help students create dioramas of the first Thanksgiving. Or, recreate the first Thanksgiving in your classroom by serving an authentic lunch.

✓ Rylant, Cynthia. *In November.* San Diego: Harcourt, Inc., 2000.

In November tells the story of what happens outdoors in the month of November. It also describes the smells, foods, and feelings of a special November day. This book is filled with beautiful, poetic language and impressionistic paintings.

December Book Selections

✓ Glaser, Linda. *The Borrowed Hanukkah Latkes.* Morton Grove, IL.: Albert Whitman & Company, 1997.

This story is about Rachel, who finds a way to include her elderly neighbor in her family's Hanukkah celebration. This book shows the value of giving from the heart. It also contains a recipe for potato latkes, a traditional Hanukkah food.

✓ Howland, Naomi. *Latkes, Latkes Good to Eat: A Chanukah Story.* New York: Clarion Books, 1999.

This is a story about Sadie and her brothers, who live in an old Russian village. They are very poor and hungry until an old woman gives Sadie a frying pan that will make potato latkes until it hears the magic words that make it stop. Students can write about a magic object that brings them everything they want. Be sure they write about the good and the bad things that could happen.

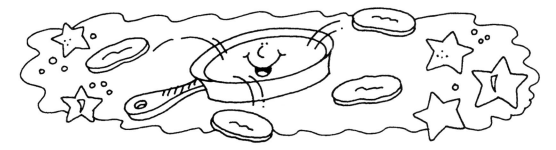

✓ Lankford, Mary D. *Christmas Around the World.* New York: Mulberry Books, 1998.

This book describes the weather, customs, decorations, foods, and traditional celebrations of Christmas in twelve different countries. The last section includes craft ideas and vocabulary definitions.

✓ Robinson, Barbara. *The Best Christmas Pageant Ever.* New York: Harper & Row Publishers, Inc., 1972.

This story portrays the unusual way an unorthodox family interprets the Christmas story. The Herdmans, the worst kids in school, learn a special message about the meaning of Christmas. Read this book as a class. You may also wish to watch the TV movie version. Discuss what the Herdmans and the other characters learn about Christmas.

✓ Thomas, Dylan. *A Child's Christmas in Wales.* New York: Holiday House, 1985.

Use this classic to show students how Christmas is celebrated in another part of the world. After reading, have students write a short paragraph about how their holiday traditions differ from those in the story.

✓ Chocolate, Deborah M. Newton. *My First Kwanzaa Book*. New York: Scholastic, 1992.

This book describes the practices of Kwanzaa through one family's celebration and is especially appropriate for younger students. To follow up, use paint-stirring sticks, construction paper, red, black, and green poster paint, and glue to make a bendera, the Kwanzaa flag.

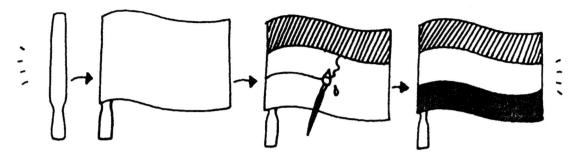

✓ Pinkney, Andrea Davis. *Seven Candles for Kwanzaa*. New York: Dial Books for Young Readers, 1993.

This book describes the origins and practices of Kwanzaa through the eyes of one family. As a class, brainstorm and then post a list of abstract nouns that would be good principles by which to live.

✓ Kindersley, Anabel. *Children Just Like Me: Celebrations!* New York: DK Publishing, Inc., 1997.

This book contains stories and photographs about holidays celebrated all over the world. The winter section is an excellent source of stories and includes information on Diwali in India, Hanukkah in the U.S., St. Nicholas Day in Slovakia, St. Lucia Day in Sweden, Christmas in Germany, and Epiphany in Spain.

January Book Selections

✓ Brett, Jan. *The Hat*. New York: Putnam Publishing Group Juvenile Books, 1997.

This story is about a young girl who hangs out her winter clothes to dry and a curious hedgehog that ends up with a stocking stuck on its head. The story ends humorously with many animals wearing articles of clothing. Follow up with students writing and/or illustrating their own stories about animals wearing funny clothing.

✓ Edwards, Richard. *Copy Me, Copycub*. New York: HarperCollins Juvenile Books, 1999.

A mother and her cub play Follow the Leader until it's time to hibernate for the winter. Have a discussion about animals that hibernate in the winter or play a game of Follow the Leader.

✓ Isadora, Rachel. *Sophie Skates*. New York: Putnam, 1999.

This books follows Sophie's dreams of becoming a professional skater. It includes factual information about skating. As a follow-up activity, have students write their own stories about becoming professional athletes.

✓ Keats, Ezra Jack. *The Snowy Day*. New York: Viking Press, 1962.

This classic, Caldecott Award-winning book tracks a little boy's day in the snow. Follow up by having students make pictures of their favorite things to do in the snow, using cut paper glued together to mimic the illustrations in the book.

✓ Neitzel, Shirley. *The Jacket I Wear in the Snow*. New York: Greenwillow, 1989.

This book tells the story of a little girl who names all the clothes she puts on to play in the snow. The story is told in a pattern similar to the "This Is the House That Jack Built" story, and the clothing words appear in rebus form. Students may act out the story by pretending to put on the clothes described or by taking turns putting on actual clothing items.

✓ Yolen, Jane. *Owl Moon*. New York: Philomel Books, 1987.

This Caldecott Award winner tells the story of a little girl and her father as they go "owling" on a cold winter night. Invite children to share special times they have spent with family or interesting things they have seen in nature.

Martin Luther King, Jr.

✓ Adler, David. *A Picture Book of Martin Luther King, Jr.* New York: Holiday House, 1989.

This book combines the main events in Martin Luther King, Jr.'s life with the turning points in his work with civil rights.

✓ Bray, Rosemary L. *Martin Luther King*. New York: Greenwillow Books, 1995.

This is a brief biography that portrays Martin Luther King, Jr. not only as a hero, but also as a human being.

✓ Marzollo, Jean. *Happy Birthday, Martin Luther King*. New York: Scholastic Trade, 1993.

This book's simple language makes it suitable for younger students. The foreword is helpful in dealing with the difficult subject of violent death and should be read before reading the book aloud to students.

February Book Selections

Valentine's Day

✓ Bulla, Clyde Robert. *The Story of Valentine's Day*. New York: HarperCollins Juvenile Books Publishers, 1999.

This book tells the history of Valentine's Day.

✓ Bunting, Eve. *The Valentine Bears*. New York: Houghton Mifflin, 1984.

This is a story about Mr. and Mrs. Bear who wake up early from their winter hibernation to share their first Valentine's Day.

✓ Marzollo, Jeane. *I Love You: A Rebus Poem.* New York: Scholastic, Inc., 2000.

The simple rhyming pattern and the rebus format in this book provide both a challenge and comfort to young readers. The pattern lends itself well to having students make up their own rhymes using the same format.

✓ Stevenson, James. *A Village Full of Valentines.* New York: Greenwillow Books, 1995.

This book includes seven short stories about animal characters living in the same village.

Black History

✓ Adler, David. *A Picture Book of Harriet Tubman.* New York: Holiday House, 1992.

This book is from a series of simply written biographies which also includes Jackie Robinson, Frederick Douglass, Rosa Parks, Martin Luther King, Jr., and Sojourner Truth.

✓ Cline-Ransome, Lesa. *Satchel Paige.* New York: Simon & Schuster, 2000.

Satchel Paige was the first African-American pitcher to play major league baseball and be inducted into the Baseball Hall of Fame. This book tells the story of his life, his talents, and his feisty personality.

✓ Pinkney, Andrea Davis. *Dear Benjamin Banneker.* San Diego: Harcourt Brace & Company, 1994.

This book tells the story of Benjamin Banneker, an African-American scientist and mathematician. Banneker was born a free man, but many people were still enslaved during his lifetime. By writing a thought-provoking letter to Thomas Jefferson, Banneker takes a stand against slavery.

✓ Hoffman, Mary. *Amazing Grace.* New York: Dial Books for Young Readers, 1991.

This is the story of Grace, who wants to play the part of Peter Pan in an upcoming school play. Her classmates tell her she can't because she is African American and a girl. In the end, she discovers she can do anything she sets her mind to do.

President's Day

✓ Adler, David A. *A Picture Book of George Washington.* New York: Holiday House, 1999.

This book is a brief telling of the life story of "The Father of Our Country."

✓ Fritz, Jean. *George Washington's Breakfast.* New York: Paper Star, 1998.

This is a story about a young and curious boy. His goal is to know all he can about George Washington, the man for whom he is named.

✓ St. George, Judith. *So You Want to Be President?* New York: Philomel Books, 2000.

This Caldecott Award-winning book is filled with comical caricatures and is the perfect read for President's Day.

✓ Waters, Kate. *The Story of the White House.* New York: Scholastic, 1992.

This is a book full of the history and trivia of the White House. It also includes interesting facts about the American presidents in the back of the book.

✓ Woods, Andrew. *Young Abraham Lincoln: Log Cabin President.* New York: Troll Associates, 1992.

This is a simply written biography of the man who was president of the United States during the Civil War.

March Book Selections

St. Patrick's Day

✓ de Paola, Tomie. *Jamie O'Rourke and the Big Potato: An Irish Folktale.* New York: G. P. Putnam, 1992.

This old Irish folktale is about the laziest man in Ireland who catches a leprechaun. The leprechaun offers a potato seed instead of gold for his freedom, and the whole community gets involved in the outcome.

✓ de Paola, Tomie. *Jamie O'Rourke and the Pooka.* New York: G. P. Putnam, 2000.

In this sequel, Jamie has four friends who visit him nightly while his wife is away. Every night, they leave a big mess, and a magical pooka cleans it up. Jamie feels he is very lucky, until his luck runs out and he learns a lesson about his laziness.

✓ Gibbons, Gail. *St. Patrick's Day.* New York: Holiday House, 1994.

This is an informational book about the life and traditions surrounding Saint Patrick.

✓ MacGill-Callahan, Sheila. *The Last Snake in Ireland: A Story about St. Patrick.* New York: Holiday House, 1999.

This story combines the famous legends of the Loch Ness monster of Scotland and that of St. Patrick driving the snakes out of Ireland.

✓ Talbott, Hudson. *O'Sullivan Stew.* New York: G. P. Putnam, 1999.

All students will enjoy this story about a girl named Kate, who saves her village on the coast of Ireland from a witch's curse.

National Nutrition Month

✓ Riccio, Nina M. *Five Kids and a Monkey Solve the Great Cupcake Caper.* Canterbury, NH: Creative Attic, 1997.

✓ Rockwell, Lizzy. *Good Enough to Eat: A Kid's Guide to Food and Nutrition.* New York: HarperCollins Juvenile Books, 1999.

Springtime/Weather

✓ Cole, Joanna. *The Magic School Bus Inside a Hurricane*. New York: Scholastic, Inc., 1995.

This book combines a fictional story with interesting facts about weather, including wind and hurricanes.

✓ Hopping, Lorraine Jean. *Wild Weather: Hurricanes*. New York: Scholastic, Inc., 1995.

This non-fiction book about hurricanes can be read aloud or enjoyed by students alone.

✓ McKissack, Patricia C. *Mirandy and Brother Wind*. New York: Alfred A. Knopf, 1988.

This Caldecott Honor book is about a girl who wants to win a cakewalk by having the wind as her partner.

✓ Shaw, Charles G. *It Looked Like Spilt Milk*. New York: Harper, 1947.

This patterned story has simple drawings of different views of clouds. Students may make their own versions with white paint on blue construction paper and compile them in a class book.

✓ Stojic, Manya. *Rain*. New York: Crown Publishers, 2000.

Illustrated with vibrant paintings, this patterned story describes the way rain feels, tastes, smells, sounds, and looks. This book is a great introduction to the five senses.

Women in History

✓ Adler, David. *A Picture Book of Helen Keller*. New York: Holiday House, 1990.

✓ Adler, David. *A Picture Book of Florence Nightingale*. New York: Holiday House, 1992.

✓ Howe, Jane Moore. *Amelia Earhart: Young Air Pioneer*. Carmel, IN: Patria Press, 1999.

✓ Parks, Rosa. *I Am Rosa Parks*. New York: Dial Books for Young Readers, 1997.

✓ Penner, Lucille Recht. *The True Story of Pocahontas*. New York: Random House, 1994.

April Book Selections

✓ Zolotow, Charlotte. *The Bunny Who Found Easter.* Boston: Houghton Mifflin Co., 1998.

This is a sweet story about a lonely rabbit who is searching for other rabbits. He meets an owl who tells him there will always be a bunny at Easter. The rabbit thinks that Easter is a place and searches through the seasons until he finally finds a special bunny and has a family of his own.

✓ Wallace, Nancy Elizabeth. *Tell-a-Bunny.* New York: Winslow Press, 2000.

Plans for a surprise birthday party change as a message gets passed from one bunny to the next, until the party is quite different from the original plan. The wonderful illustrations in this book are made from cut paper, which would be fun for your students to try as an art-project technique.

✓ Desmoinaux, Christel. *Mrs. Hen's Big Surprise.* New York: Margaret K. McElderry Books, 2000.

Mrs. Hen finds a big egg in her garden. She sits on it and dreams of her life with her new baby. This story will appeal to kindergartners and first graders. Have them predict what is in the egg before you reveal it in the book.

✓ Joyce, William. *Bently and Egg.* New York: Laura Geringer Books, 1999.

A shy, singing frog is left in charge of an egg, which he decorates. When the egg is mistaken for an Easter egg, it is "eggnapped." The experience changes the frog's life forever. Use this book as a springboard into a discussion about feelings.

✓ Walton, Rick. *One More Bunny: Adding from One to Ten.* New York: HarperCollins Publishers, 2000.

This is a book of counting and addition. Illustrations show different combinations for each value. Children will enjoy finding and counting a variety of items, such as butterflies and bees. This is a great book for a math center.

✓ Gibbons, Gail. *Rabbits, Rabbits, and More Rabbits.* New York: Holiday House, 2000.

This nonfiction book describes different kinds of rabbits: their physical characteristics, behavior, where they live, and how to care for pet rabbits. It is full of interesting information and colorful illustrations.

✓ Zolotow, Charlotte. *Mr. Rabbit and the Lovely Present.* New York: Harper & Row, 1962.

A little girl seeks the help of Mr. Rabbit to find a present for her mother. Mr. Rabbit helps her create a lovely present made up of several favorite colors. This book presents a nice exploration of color. It can be tied into science or art activities.

✓ Ray, Mary Lyn. *Red Rubber Boot Day.* San Diego: Harcourt, Inc., 2000.

This book follows the path of a boy inside and out on a rainy day.

✓ Dorros, Arthur. *The Fungus That Ate My School.* New York: Scholastic Press, 2000.

This is a story about a fungus experiment that grows and takes over the school during a rainy spring vacation. Students will love the vibrant illustrations and humor.

✓ Spier, Peter. *Peter Spier's Rain.* Garden City, N.Y.: Doubleday & Company, Inc., 1982.

A wordless book, this classic shows the activities of a brother and sister during a rainstorm. It is wonderful for both young children, who can tell the story as they look at the pictures, and for older children, who can write stories to match the illustrations.

✓ Barrett, Judi. *Cloudy with a Chance of Meatballs.* New York: Aladdin Books, 1982.

This humorous story tells about a town where it rains food. Each day, the people of the town of Chewandswallow listen to the weather forecast to learn what they'll be eating that day. Students will appreciate the illustrations, which will motivate them to create their own weather forecasts for the town of Chewandswallow. Ask them to write stories about other types of strange weather, such as rain made of cotton balls or pennies.

✓ Cole, Joanna. *The Magic School Bus at the Waterworks.* New York: Scholastic Inc., 1986.

Explore a combination of facts about water, clouds, what makes it rain, and the water cycle with Ms. Frizzle as the guide.

✓ Branley, Franklyn. *Down Comes the Rain.* New York: HarperCollins Publishers, 1997.

A nonfiction introduction to weather and the water cycle is told in simple terms, with colorful illustrations that will appeal to kindergartners and first graders. Many hands-on activities are also suggested. This is a great book to include in a science center.

Earth Day

✓ Asch, Frank. *The Earth and I.* San Diego: Gulliver Books, 1994.

This book shows the friendship between a boy and nature, as they care for each other and help each other grow.

✓ Gibbons, Gail. *Recycle: A Handbook for Kids.* Boston: Little Brown & Co., 1992.

Follow the paths of five different types of garbage that are collected for recycling. The book shows how recycled materials can be converted into new products. This is a good springboard book for a class recycling project.

✓ Madden, Don. *The Wartville Wizard.* New York: Aladdin Books, 1993.

This is a story about an old man who fights a town of litterbugs by magically sending each piece of trash back to the person who dropped it. The town learns a lesson about keeping things clean. Follow up by sending your class out to pick up trash on the playground or another area surrounding the school. Encourage students to make plans for an ongoing cleanup project, such as having two students designated each week for the job.

✓ Cherry, Lynne. *The Great Kapok Tree: A Tale of the Amazon Rain Forest.* San Diego: Harcourt Brace Jovanovich, 1990.

This story of conservation is about the many different animals that live in a great kapok tree in the Brazilian rain forest. One by one, the animals try to convince a man with an ax to preserve their home. The book contains beautiful illustrations and an introduction with rain forest facts.

✓ Seuss, Dr. *The Lorax.* New York: Random House, 1971.

This classic Dr. Seuss story is about the Once-ler, who describes the effects of the local pollution problem that resulted from his own greediness. You can use this book as a lead-in to a discussion on how pollution affects real animals.

✓ Udry, Janice May. *A Tree Is Nice.* New York: Harper, 1956.

A Caldecott Medal winner, this book is about the good things that trees provide. Have your students write their own ideas about trees, following the same pattern as the book: "A tree is nice because. . ." Compile student sentences and illustrations into a class book.

May and June Book Selections

Gardening

✓ Cooney, Barbara. *Miss Rumphius.* New York: Viking Press, 1982.

This story is about Alice Rumphius, a woman who fulfilled a promise she made to her grandfather to do something to make the world more beautiful.

✓ Heller, Ruth. *The Reason for a Flower.* New York: Price Stern Sloan Publishing, 1983.

This is a nonfiction book about flowers. The information is presented in rhyme and is complemented by beautiful illustrations.

✓ Lobel, Anita. *Alison's Zinnia.* New York: Greenwillow Books, 1990.

This book features a flower for every letter of the alphabet.

✓ Stewart, Sarah. *The Gardener.* New York: HarperCollins, 1997.

This book contains a series of letters relating what happens when Lydia Grace goes to live in the city with her Uncle Jim after her father loses his job. Her love of gardening serves as a comfort to her during the difficult time.

✓ Van Allsburg, Chris. *The Garden of Abdul Gasazi.* Boston: Houghton Mifflin Company, 1979.

This story is about a boy named Alan who is caring for a dog that runs away into the forbidden garden of a retired magician.

May Day

✓ Mora, Pat. *The Rainbow Tulip.* New York: Viking Children's Books, 1999.

A Mexican-American girl experiences the difficulties and joy of being different when she wears a tulip costume for the school May Day parade.

Cinco de Mayo

✓ Menard, Valerie. *The Latino Holiday Book: From Cinco de Mayo to Dia de Los Muertos: The Celebrations and Traditions of Hispanic-Americans.* New York: Marlowe and Company, 2000.

✓ Palacios, Argentina. *Viva Mexico! The Story of Benito Juarez and Cinco de Mayo.* Austin: Raintree/Steck-Vaughn, 1996.

✓ Vazquez, Sarah. *A World of Holidays—Cinco de Mayo.* Austin: Raintree/Steck-Vaughn, 1999.

Mothers and Fathers

✓ Bunting, Eve. *A Perfect Father's Day.* New York: Clarion Books, 1993.

A four-year-old girl plans the perfect day, full of her father's favorite activities.

✓ Joffe Numeroff, Laura. *What Mommies Do Best/What Daddies Do Best.* New York: Simon & Schuster, 1998.

Two stories in one are presented in this book. One features a mother as the main character, and the other features a father.

✓ Neitzel, Shirley. *We're Making Breakfast for Mother.* New York: Greenwillow Books, 1997.

Rhymes and rebuses show children making breakfast for their mother; told in a pattern similar to the classic "This is the house that Jack built. . ."

✓ Smalls-Hector, Irene. *Kevin and His Dad.* Boston: Little, Brown, and Company, 1999.

Kevin spends an entire wonderful day working and playing with his father.

✓ Zolotow, Charlotte. *This Quiet Lady.* New York: Greenwillow Books, 1992.

A child finds out about her mother's early life by looking at old pictures.

Flag Day

✓ Ryan, Pam Muñoz. *The Flag We Love.* Watertown, MA: Charlesbridge, 1996.

This book is a poetic tribute to the American flag and describes the different meanings behind this enduring symbol.

Poetry Sources

Choral Readings

A great way to get students interested in poetry and to help develop reading fluency is by doing choral readings. A choral reading is when a selection is read aloud by a group of students. At first, the readings should be done as a class. When the students are more familiar with the piece, the teacher may assign parts to smaller groups. Here are suggested methods for choral reading.

1. Put a copy of a poem on an overhead projector for students to read.

2. Give a "poem of the week" to the students on Monday and use it for choral readings throughout the week. On Friday, students may have a chance to read the poem alone or in a small group. They may want to be creative with their presentation by acting the poem out in some way, possibly using props.

3. Give copies of several poems to students at the beginning of the month. The leader of the day chooses the poem to read each day.

4. Incorporate poetry that has a theme to go along with other content areas, such as math, science, or social studies.

Fall Themes

✓ Carlstrom, Nancy White. *Thanksgiving Day at Our House: Thanksgiving Poems for the Very Young.* New York: Simon & Schuster Books for Young Readers, 1999.

✓ Dakos, Kalli. *If You're Not Here, Please Raise Your Hand: Poems About School.* New York: Four Winds Press, 1990.

✓ Prelutsky, Jack. *It's Halloween.* New York: Greenwillow Books, 1977.

✓ Prelutsky, Jack. *It's Thanksgiving.* New York: Greenwillow Books, 1982.

✓ Prelutsky, Jack. *The New Kid on the Block: Poems.* New York: Greenwillow Books, 1984.

✓ Sierra, Judy. *There's a Zoo in Room 22.* San Diego: Harcourt, Inc., 2000.

Winter Themes

✓ Bauer, Caroline Feller, ed. *Snowy Day Stories and Poems.* New York: HarperCollins, 1987.

This collection includes poems by Eve Merriam and Ogden Nash, short stories from Russia and Japan, and recipes for snow muffins and snow pudding.

✓ Prelutsky, Jack. *It's Valentine's Day.* New York: Scholastic, 1983.

This is a collection of humorous valentine poems and rhymes.

✓ Rogasky, Barbara, comp. *Winter Poems.* New York: Scholastic, 1994.

This collection features a variety of poems, including works by William Shakespeare, Robert Frost, Emily Dickinson, and Carl Sandburg.

✓ Siddals, Mary McKenna. *Millions of Snowflakes.* New York: Clarion Books, 1998.

This is a poem about a child anticipating a snowfall and plans for outdoor fun.

✓ Sierra, Judy. *Antarctic Antics.* San Diego: Harcourt Brace & Company, 1998.

This book is filled with humorous penguin poems.

Spring/Summer Themes

✓ Baker, Keith. *Big Fat Hen.* San Diego: Harcourt Brace & Co., 1994.

This book contains colorful illustrations for the nursery rhyme "One, Two, Buckle My Shoe." It makes a nice choral reading for kindergartners or first graders.

✓ Florian, Doug. *On the Wing.* San Diego: Harcourt Brace & Co., 1996.

April is a great month for bird watching. Bright watercolors complement the humorous verses about different birds in this book.

✓ Hoberman, Mary Ann. *Fathers, Mothers, Sisters, Brothers.* Boston: Little Brown and Company, 1991.

This collection of family poems is perfect for celebrating Mother's Day and Father's Day.

✓ Kennedy, X.J. and Dorothy M. Kennedy, eds. *Talking Like the Rain: A Read-To-Me Book of Poems.* Boston: Little Brown & Co., 1992.

This book has a wide collection of poetry, including some on wind and weather, and some about families.

✓ Lansky, Bruce, comp. *No More Homework! No More Tests!: Kids' Favorite Funny School Poems.* New York: Meadowbrook Press, 1997.

Celebrate the end of the school year with poems about school.

✓ Prelutsky, Jack, ed. *The Random House Book of Poetry for Children.* New York: Random House, 1983.

This book is organized by themes, such as nature, seasons, animals, children, and food. It's a classic anthology, filled with the best in children's poetry.

✓ Prelutsky, Jack, ed. *Read-Aloud Rhymes for the Very Young.* New York: Alfred Knopf, 1986.

This book contains poems on many familiar subjects and is nicely organized by theme. The verses are simple and fun. You'll find choral reading on almost any subject here.

✓ Wing, Natasha. *The Night Before Easter.* New York: Grosset & Dunlap, 1999.

This take-off on the famous Christmas poem works well for a choral reading.

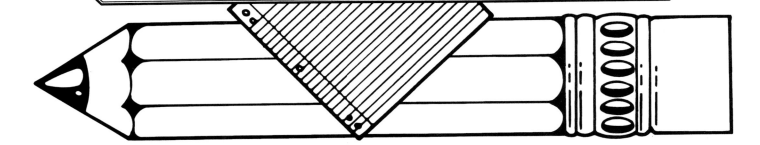

Math Activities

How Many Are Hidden?

~~~ **Objective:** **Students demonstrate their understanding of numbers.**

~~~ **Materials:** Ten small objects, all the same (pennies, paper clips)

~~~ **Procedure:**
1. Use some or all of the ten small objects. Sit facing the student. Scramble and count the objects along with the student.

2. Scramble the objects once more but this time cover some with your hand.

3. Have the student count the visible objects and then tell how many must be hidden by your hand. (With three objects, you will hide zero, one, two, and three, but not in predictable order. With four objects, you will hide zero, one, two, three, and four, but again not in predictable order.)

Helpful Hint!

Begin with two objects. If the student gives the correct answers, move up to three objects. Continue adding an object until the student no longer answers correctly. Random guesses indicate that the student has moved beyond his or her understanding.

Recognition without Counting

~~~ **Objective:**   **Students recognize numbers of objects up to ten without counting.**

~~~ **Materials:**   Multiple flashcards for all whole numbers up to 10, each shown with several different arrangements of dots

~~~ **Procedure:**

1. Have the students call out the total number of dots on each card. Begin with cards showing 1 through 3 only. Add higher numbers as students become proficient.

2. Keep at this until students recognize all amounts to 10 without counting.

This activity prepares students for addition and subtraction, since they see that different groups of dots can make up the same number. For example, they see that 5 can be $4 + 1$, $2 + 3$, $2 + 1 + 2$, and so on.

Helpful Hint!

Encourage students to play jacks. When the jacks scatter, students must pick them up in unpredictable configurations of numbers.

Card Games

~~~ **Objective:**   **Students increase their ability to do mental math.**

~~~ **Materials:**   Many sets of old playing cards, even incomplete decks (with all face cards removed)

~~~ **Procedure:**   **Game 1** (two students): Separate the cards into two equal piles, one for each player. Each player flips over a card, and the highest (or lowest) card wins. The winner of the round takes both cards. Play continues until all cards are used up. The player with the most cards wins. (This game can be played very fast, as fast as students can recognize numbers.)

Game 2 (two students): Separate the cards into two piles (as above). Each player flips over a card and must add (or multiply) the numbers on the cards. The first player to say the correct answer aloud takes all the cards. (For this activity, have a third student judge correct answers.)

Fact Families Game

〜〜 **Objective:**

Students increase their ability to use the three numbers and four combinations of any fact family.

For example:

3 + 4 = 7; 4 + 3 = 7; 7 − 3 = 4; 7 − 4 = 3

〜〜 **Materials:**

Deck of playing cards, face cards removed (each ace is read as 1)

〜〜 **Procedure:**

1. In this game, players attempt to collect sets of three cards that make appropriate fact families. A player who, for example, collect 3, 4, and 7 can put the cards down as a set but must also tell the four combinations that the numbers make.

2. The game is played like Go Fish. Each player is dealt seven cards. The rest of the deck is placed between them.

3. On his or her turn, each player requests a specific card from another player (for example, "Ann, do you have a 3?"). If the player gets the card that he or she asked for, then he or she plays the cards and gets another turn.

4. If the player does not get the desired card, he or she must "go fish" by drawing a card from the deck. Play then continues with the next player.

Helpful Hint!

Older students may play using multiplication and division. They may also collect four or five cards in order to show double- or triple-digit numbers.

For example:

18 can be shown as 3 × 6, 10 + 8, or 9 + 9.

Kids' Own Word Problems

〜〜 **Objective:** **Students understand multiplication by relating it to objects in their environment.**

〜〜 **Materials:** Chart paper, labeled *Things That Come in Twos, Things That Come in Threes,* and so on

Old magazines and newspapers

Scissors

Glue

〜〜 **Procedure:**
1. Students brainstorm objects that naturally come in sets of two, three, four, or whichever tables you are learning.

2. Students cut out pictures of these objects from old magazines and paste them on the appropriate chart. (If students can't find the pictures in magazines or newspapers, they can draw them.)

3. Students then write word problems based on the charts.

4. Copy and bind the word problems in groups of five and hand them out as classwork or homework.

Times Tables Display

〜〜 **Objective:**   **Students visualize the multiplication tables.**

〜〜 **Materials:**   Manipulatives that connect easily (paper clips, Unifix cubes), in ten different colors, with increasing totals of each color

For example:

Ones	= 10 blue paper clips		Sixes	= 60 brown paper clips
Twos	= 20 yellow paper clips		Sevens	= 70 black paper clips
Threes	= 30 red paper clips		Eights	= 80 orange paper clips
Fours	= 40 green paper clips		Nines	= 90 pink paper clips
Fives	= 50 purple paper clips		Tens	= 100 white paper clips

Posterboard

Glue or tape

Marker

〜〜 **Procedure:**

1. Hook the manipulatives together according to the numbers they represent. For example, hook the red paper clips into groups of three; hook the black paper clips into groups of 7; blue paper clips will not be hooked together, since they represent 1.

2. Mount the paperclips onto tagboard according to color. Each tagboard should show ten groups of paper clips.

3. Label the tagboards with the numbers they represent. Also label each row of paper clips.

4. Show students how to count the paper clips to demonstrate multiplication facts.

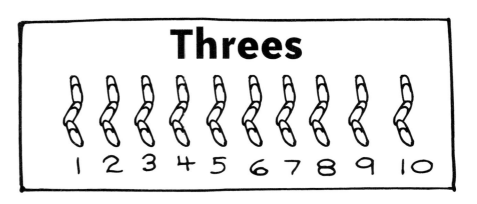

Math Bingo

〜〜 Objective: **Students practice computation in a game setting.**

〜〜 Materials: Bingo grids with number of squares appropriate to grade level—either 9, 16, or 25 squares

Bucket, hat, or similar container (to hold math problems)

Slips of paper with math problems (any process) written on them

A list of answers

Scrap paper and pencils

〜〜 Procedure:

1. Place math problems in the bucket.

2. Place corresponding answers on the board.

3. Give students a specific amount of time to copy the answers from the board into any of the squares on their bingo grids.

4. Pull a problem out of the bucket and read it aloud. Students work the problem in their minds or on paper and draw an X over the corresponding answer on their grids.

5. Draw more problems from the bucket and follow the procedure in Step 4.

6. As students call out "Bingo!" you may reward them with pencils, stickers, stamps, or similar prizes.

Roll' Em!

~~~ Objective: **Students attempt to get the highest possible scores by using a variety of math computations and processes.**

~~~ Materials: Five dice (game can also be played in small groups; each group would then need its own set of dice)

Four index cards per student, each labeled with a process sign: $+$, $-$, $\times$, $\div$

Paper and pencils

~~~ Procedure:
1. Roll the dice and write the five numbers rolled on the board.

2. Students decide where to place process cards (one between each number on the board) to compute the highest possible number as an answer.

3. Do not ask students to write out their computations—that takes all of the fun out of it! If they forget how they got their totals, have them keep trying until they get the totals again. The answer is not as important as the fun of problem solving. Gradually, students will develop strategies and learn to multiply by the largest number and divide by the smallest.

4. Ask students to raise their hands and announce their high scores. Or, to keep the answers secret, have students write their answers on paper and hold them up for only the teacher to see. Give a signal if a student shows the highest possible answer. If the students haven't reached the highest answer, encourage them to keep trying!

Helpful Hint!

This activity can be done with three dice and two processes, four dice and three processes, or five dice and all four processes. It can also be simplified, if necessary, to accommodate your students' ability levels.

Hop around the Clock

〜〜 **Objective:** Students move their bodies around a large floor clock and get a physical "sense" of time and how to read a clock.

〜〜 **Materials:** Twelve rubber pads or cardboard squares, approximately 12″ (30.5 cm) square, numbered 1–12 (cardboard will need masking tape to stay in place)

Two lengths of rope (hour and minute hands for floor clock)

〜〜 **Procedure:**

Sixty Minutes

1. Place the pads on the ground to represent the numbers on a clock, but place them facedown. Doing this eliminates the initial confusion of, for example, seeing the 2 and having to call it "ten."

2. Begin by teaching that an hour has sixty minutes.

3. Count out the entire sixty minutes as you and/or a child walk around the clock, being sure that you are in the correct spot when arriving at five, ten, fifteen, and so on.

Counting by Fives

1. Instead of counting out all numbers around the clock, students count by fives to sixty.

2. Have the students start walking around the squares in rhythm, counting by fives. Students take turns and must jump both feet onto the pad while saying the number. The rhythm will be as follows: step, step, five; step, step, ten; step, step, fifteen.

Five-Minute Hop

1. Ask a student questions such as "Can you hop to ten?" and "Can you hop to thirty-five?" The student should then perform the requested move to the designated pad.

2. When the students have mastered finding fives on the clock with pads facedown, turn the pads over so that the numbers show and continue with the activity.

Now You Are Ready to Tell Time!

1. Explain the following to students:

   Big hand—This hand counts the minutes. The big hand is the boss and encourages the little hand to move. When the big hand has landed on 12, then the little hand points to the new number (hour).

Hop around the Clock (continued)

Little hand—This hand names the hour. The little hand is short-sighted and can't even see the next number until it is right on top of it.

2. Make a clock by placing the numbers in a large circle on the floor.

3. Have students line up in groups of three to the left of the clock.

4. Stand in the center of the clock, holding two ropes of different lengths. The short one will be the "hour" rope, and the long one will be the "minute" rope.

5. Have a group of three students enter the clock. Have one student pick up the hour rope and another pick up the minute rope.

6. Tell the third student a time. He or she should adjust the positions of the other two students to the specified time as they hold onto their ropes.

7. After the first group completes the task correctly, they exit the circle to the right and the next group enters the circle from the left.

How Much Money Is There Today?

~~~ **Objective:** **Students practice showing coin amounts in a variety of ways.**

~~~ **Materials:** Large pocket chart with clear see-through pockets.

Four labeled containers holding pennies, nickels, dimes, and quarters (preferably large play money that can be seen easily by the class)

~~~ **Procedure:**
1. Write the date on the board (for example, January 23). Or, you may write it on a sentence strip and place it in the top pocket of the chart.

2. Ask a student to come to the pocket chart and show one way to make twenty-three cents. Continue with more students until all coin combinations have been exhausted.

3. Write more dates on the board and invite students to make the coin combinations for the class.

Counting Coins

~~~ **Objective:** **Students get hands-on practice determining the value of coins.**

~~~ **Materials:** Overhead projector

Overhead coins (made for use with an overhead projector)

Play money (cardboard or plastic coins)

~~~ **Procedure:**
1. Place a random pile of coins on the overhead projector.

2. Have the students verbally help you divide the pile into coin groups, noting visual differences in size, color, and characteristics of heads and tails. Ask the students what distinguishes one coin from another. (Students often confuse quarters and nickels, since they are the same color and similar in size.)

3. Next, have the students compare the value of each coin group. Count the coins with the largest value first (quarters), then the next lowest value (dimes), and so on.

4. Show the students various coin groups that make up the value of another coin. For example, five pennies equal one nickel, two dimes and a nickel equal one quarter, and so on.

5. After doing this activity several times as a class, students should be able to do it on their own, working with partners and play money. They can challenge each other to make various coin combinations for specific amounts. (For example, "How many different ways can you make ten cents?" "What is the most amount of coins you can use for fifty cents?" "What is the least amount of coins you can use for fifty cents?")

Circle of Months and Seasons

~~~ **Objective:**

Students identify months of the year with numbers on a clock. By using a circle, they also see that months (and seasons) go around and come back again.

~~~ **Materials:**

36" (91.5 cm) diameter circle made of paper, felt, or flannel, with a moveable hand fastened to the center

Twelve construction paper rectangles (about 3" × 12", 7.5 cm × 30.5 cm), each labeled with the name of a month

~~~ **Procedure:**

Circle of Months

1. Place the first rectangle (January) on the circle where 1 is located on a clock face. Continue placing months around the circle in the appropriate places (February at 2 o'clock, March at 3 o'clock, and so on, ending with December at 12 o'clock).

2. At the beginning of each month, move the hand to point to the correct month on the "clock."

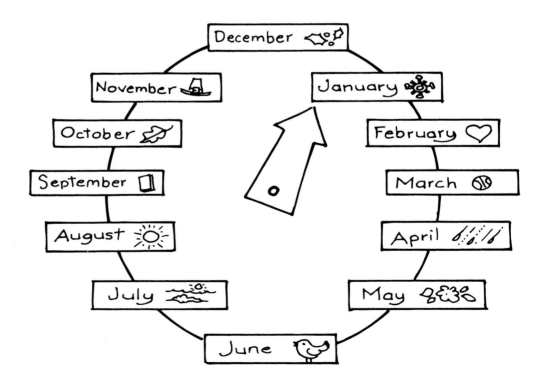

Circle of Months and Seasons (continued)

Circle of Seasons

This circle of months can also be made to show the change of seasons.

1. In this case, you will need four different colors with which to make the month-name rectangles. For example: pale blue for winter, pale green for spring, yellow for summer, and orange for autumn.

2. Eight months are solid colors since they fall within one season.

   January, February—blue

   April, May—green

   July, August—yellow

   October, November—orange

3. Four months have a season change during the month and therefore need two colors.

   March (winter/spring)—blue/green

   June (spring/summer)—green/yellow

   September (summer/autumn)—yellow/orange

   December (autumn/winter)—orange/blue

Fraction Strips

~~~ **Objective:**

Students make their own fraction strips to use as tangible fraction models.

Materials:

Four 1" × 12" (2.5 cm × 20.25 cm) different-colored construction paper strips per student

Scissors

Rulers

Pencils

Manila envelopes (to hold strips)

Procedure:

1. Have each student take one strip of paper and label it *One whole = 1.*

2. Have each student take another strip, measure it with a ruler, and cut it in half. Tell students to label each half *One-half = 1/2.*

3. Have each student take a third strip, measure it in fourths, and cut it into four equal parts. Tell students to label each part *One-fourth = 1/4.*

4. The final strip presents more difficulty. Have students work with their rulers to determine how big pieces should be to cut the strip into thirds. Tell students not to cut until you have checked their measurements. After they have correctly cut their strips into thirds, have them label each part *One-third = 1/3.*

5. Have the students store their fraction strips in manila envelopes. The strips can be taken out and used during fraction lessons, allowing students to make comparisons.

All strips should not be cut on the same day. Students should cut one set of fraction strips per day, discussing the concepts of *one whole, one-half, one-fourth,* and *one-third* and then comparing the strips to other objects in the classroom.

As students become more advanced in their study of fractions, they may add more strips to their envelopes, such as fifths, sixths, and eighths.

Drawing Fractions

Students understand and visualize written fractions.

~~~ **Materials:**

Large dice, two pair (any size will work, but large dice make the game more fun)

~~~ **Procedure:**

1. Divide the class into two equal teams. If there are an odd number of students in your class, you may play on a team or ask a student to take a turn on each team.

2. To begin, two students from each team go to the board. One student from each pair rolls the dice and the other writes on the board.

3. Students write the first number rolled as the denominator. The second number rolled is the numerator.

4. Each pair then discusses how to draw pictures of their fractions. See examples below:

$$\frac{4}{1} \qquad\qquad \frac{2}{5} \qquad\qquad \frac{6}{3}$$

5. Involve the entire class. As pairs from each team work at the board, other team members draw their own fraction ideas at their desks. Students can share ideas to decide which drawing creates the best visualization for each fraction.

6. Each team must decide which fraction is the larger number. When students are first learning fractions, one-sixth may sound bigger than one-third. This activity is a good way to help students actually visualize fractions.

Drop-Out Game

~~~ **Objective:**   **Students practice reading place value in large numbers, naming both numbers and commas. They will also learn basic probability.**

~~~ **Materials:**   Number tiles 0–9

Small box or other container (to hold tiles)

Paper and pencils

~~~ **Procedure:**   The object of this game is to build the biggest (or smallest) possible number with number tiles drawn from the box.

1. To begin, draw three lines on the board and label them *hundreds, tens,* and *ones*. Have the students do the same on their papers.

2. Draw a number tile from the box and ask students, "Where shall we place this number in order to end up with the biggest possible number?" For example, if you draw the number 3, students may initially want to place it randomly on any of the lines.

3. Discuss how the value of the 3 changes depending on where it is placed. Say, "In the ones place, it is only three things, but in the hundreds place, it changes to three hundred things!" Students will say that 300 is bigger than 3, so place the 3 in the hundreds place.

4. Now talk about probability. What are the odds that a larger digit will come out of the box? If you have drawn the 3, the odds favor that a 4, 5, 6, 7, 8, or 9 will come out next time instead of a 2 or 1.

5. To get the biggest possible number, students must decide where to place the 3 with probabilities in mind. Gradually, they begin to realize that to get the biggest number, they should probably place the 3 in the ones place and save the other lines for bigger numbers that will probably be drawn afterward.

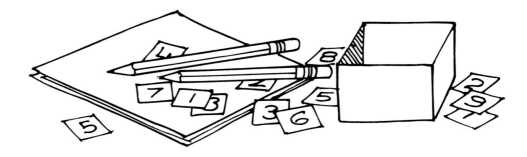

Drop-Out Game (continued)

6. Students have the option of dropping one number (if three lines are on the board, draw four numbers). Students will soon see that if they are trying to build the biggest possible number, they should drop a 1 or 0; and later, when they are trying to build the smallest number, they should drop an 8 or a 9.

Have the class do this activity frequently until students demonstrate a good understanding of the method. Later, students can play the game individually, with each student making personal choices on his or her own "game board." Students then read their numbers aloud, "winning" if it is indeed the biggest (or smallest) possible number with the given digits.

Gradually add more lines. With four lines, add the appropriate comma, telling students that they never have to read anything higher than hundreds, but that they do have to learn what the comma stands for (thousand, million, and so on). You may begin by labeling the comma and reading the numbers aloud for students.

For example:

"Three thousand, six hundred ninety-seven."

<u> 3 </u>, <u> 6 </u> <u> 9 </u> <u> 7 </u>
    thousand

Falling Down the Hill

~~~ **Objective:**

Students learn to round off any number.

~~~ **Materials:**

Butcher paper, approximately 1' × 10' (0.3 m × 3.0 m) for class chart

Markers

Make the chart as follows:

For each foot (0.3 m) of length, draw a hill. Going up each hill on the left, write the numbers *1, 2, 3,* and *4.* Leave the top of each hill blank. Going down each hill on the right, write *5, 6, 7, 8,* and *9.* Underneath the points where the hills join, write *10, 20,* and so on up to *100.* (See illustration below.) Laminate the chart and display it in the classroom where all students can see it.

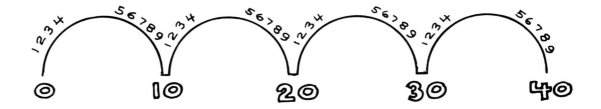

~~~ **Procedure:**

Use the chart to teach the concept of rounding off.

1. For students to round off the numbers *1, 2, 3,* and *4,* tell them that they must slide backward down the hill to the smaller of the tens.

2. For students to round off the numbers *5, 6, 7, 8,* and *9,* tell them that they must slide forward down the hill to the larger of the tens.

Helpful Hint!

Make a small individual chart for each student. These charts may be kept in students' math books or taped right to their desks. Students may use these charts as references when rounding off numbers.

Which Way Will the Wagon Roll?

〜〜 Objective: **Students use the concept of a rolling wagon to round off numbers.**

〜〜 Materials:

Chart paper

Construction paper, several colors

Scissors

Markers

Make the chart as follows:

Draw a large hill on the chart paper. Write the numbers *1–10* along the curve of the hill, spacing the numbers so that *4* is just before the peak of the hill and *5* is slightly past the peak (see illustration below). Make a wagon from construction paper and hold it on the chart above the hill.

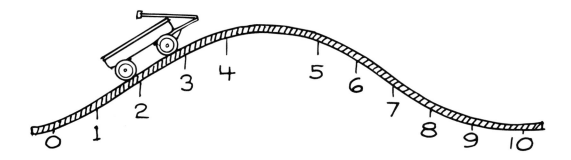

〜〜 Procedure:

1. Ask the students questions such as the following, while demonstrating with the wagon on the chart: "If we pull the wagon up to the 3 and then let it go, which way will it roll?" "What if we push the wagon up to the 4 and let go? Which way will it roll?" "Watch out now! What if we push the wagon over the hill to the 5 and let go? Now which way will it roll?"

2. When the students understand numbers at this level, you can change the beginning and ending numbers to tens or any other set and continue asking the same basic questions. New numbers can be added or removed by writing them on sticky notes.

Helpful Hint!

You may want to attach Velcro pieces over the numbers and onto the back of the wagon. Then you can stick the wagon to the chart without holding it.

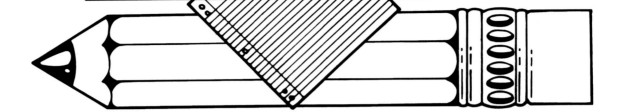

Arts and Crafts Activities

A Class Totem Pole

After discussing the history of totem poles of early America, make your own class totem pole to tell the story of each person in the class. Each student should choose an animal with which he or she has some characteristic in common. After drawing or tracing their animals, students can mount them on different-colored and different-shaped paper. Under their animals, have students explain the symbolic connection between themselves and the animals they chose. All animals are then mounted on top of each other vertically and displayed for all to read and enjoy.

Examples

1. The butterfly is a good symbol for me because I like to travel a lot.

2. The peacock is a good symbol for me because I like to show off or perform for others.

3. The lion is a good symbol for me because I'm a good leader.

Egg Carton Totem Poles

Supplies:

• cardboard egg cartons (with the egg sections cut into two strips of six; one strip for each student)

• markers or tempera paints

• glue

• scissors

Directions for students:

Using markers or paint, design and decorate the "totem pole." Use the lids of the egg cartons to cut out wings, horns, hands, or ears. Glue them onto the totem pole. (The lids can also be used as bases for the totem poles.) Allow the totem pole to dry thoroughly.

Collage of . . .

Take students outside to gather up small twigs and branches. Clean these off with paper towels for the art project. Provide scraps of art paper, yarn, tissue paper—any type of materials that might be used to create flowers on the twigs and branches. Tell students to use their imaginations and create beautiful flowers.

Wood Name Blocks

Instruct students to spell their names with the alphabet macaroni. Then have students glue their name onto a wood block. (Lumberyards will cut small squares of wood, or they can be ordered from art supply stores.) If students would like their names in color, instruct them to press lightly with a magic marker over the top of the macaroni. Name blocks can then be varnished for a finished look.

Stained-Glass Windows

First, make a frame from posterboard. Punch two holes at the top to thread yarn or ribbon through as a hanger. Give each student a sheet of waxed paper and white glue. Cut small squares of colorful tissue paper and glue these, overlapping them sightly, onto the waxed paper. After this dries completely, cut the sheet to fit behind the frame. Tape the "stained glass" in place. Hang this in a bright place for the sun to shine through.

Bookmark That Holds!

Materials
- wallpaper, cut into strips (about 2" × 9" [5 × 23 cm]).
- self-stick flat magnets
- laminating fill or contact paper

Directions

Glue or stick two magnets at the inside bottom of the strip, one on each end. Fold strips in half. (You may want to laminate the cut strips.)

The bookmark should be placed at the top or side of a page of a book so that the magnets hold together.

The bookmarks can be personalized any way students choose and make great gifts for the holidays.

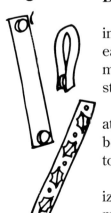

Apple Windows

Duplicate two apple patterns on red, green, or yellow construction paper for each student. Make sure each apple pattern has an inner line drawn around it approximately 3/4" from the outside edge. Have students cut out the center of each apple using the inner line as a guide. This will make an apple-shaped frame. Use the apple center as a pattern to cut two pieces of waxed paper, except cut waxed paper 1/4" (.6 cm) larger all the way around.

Have students shave crayon bits onto one of the pieces of waxed paper using a crayon sharpener, potato peeler, or a plastic knife; or you could do crayon shavings ahead of time and put each color into separate containers. Cover the shavings with the other piece of waxed paper. With a towel underneath and on top of the waxed paper, iron the papers together so the crayon shavings melt. Glue one apple frame to the waxed paper. Match up the second apple and glue to the other side so the waxed paper is sandwiched between the apple frames.

Hang apples from the ceiling on lights, or tape to walls or bulletin boards. Apple windows are displayed best when hung in a window where students can enjoy all the colors when the sun shines through the melted crayon.

Variation: Sandwich a piece of colored (red, green, or yellow) tissue paper or cellophane between two apple-shaped frames.

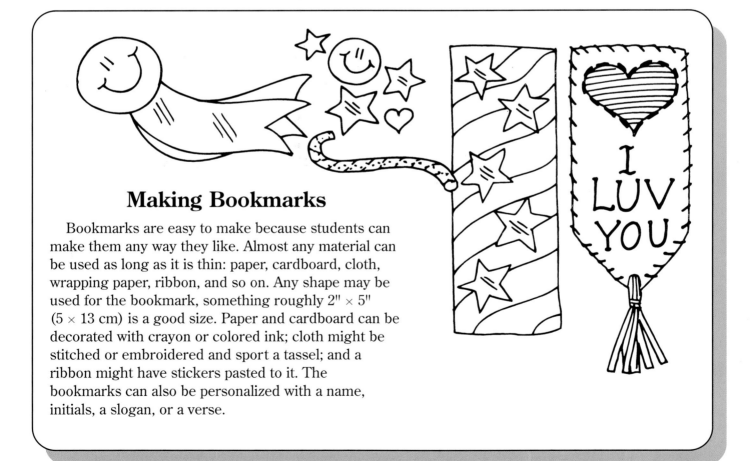

Making Bookmarks

Bookmarks are easy to make because students can make them any way they like. Almost any material can be used as long as it is thin: paper, cardboard, cloth, wrapping paper, ribbon, and so on. Any shape may be used for the bookmark, something roughly 2" × 5" (5 × 13 cm) is a good size. Paper and cardboard can be decorated with crayon or colored ink; cloth might be stitched or embroidered and sport a tassel; and a ribbon might have stickers pasted to it. The bookmarks can also be personalized with a name, initials, a slogan, or a verse.

Orange-Peel Bird Feeder

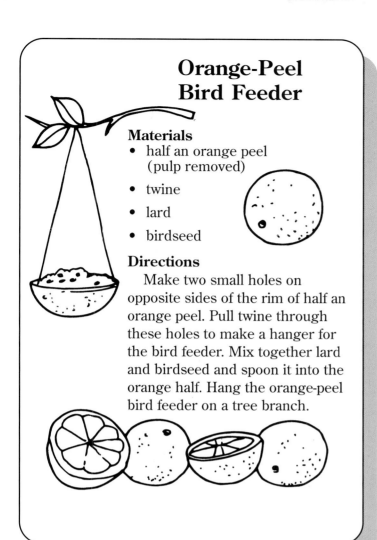

Materials
- half an orange peel (pulp removed)
- twine
- lard
- birdseed

Directions

Make two small holes on opposite sides of the rim of half an orange peel. Pull twine through these holes to make a hanger for the bird feeder. Mix together lard and birdseed and spoon it into the orange half. Hang the orange-peel bird feeder on a tree branch.

A Letter Holder

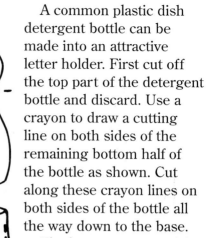

A common plastic dish detergent bottle can be made into an attractive letter holder. First cut off the top part of the detergent bottle and discard. Use a crayon to draw a cutting line on both sides of the remaining bottom half of the bottle as shown. Cut along these crayon lines on both sides of the bottle all the way down to the base.

The base structure of the letter holder is finished. Decorate the letter holder with acrylic paint or punch holes around the edges with a paper punch and weave yarn through the holes.

Detergent-Bottle Bird Feeder

Materials
- plastic dish-detergent bottle
- small dowel
- twine
- birdseed

Directions

Wash and dry an empty plastic detergent bottle. Cut a hole on each side of the bottle that is big enough for a bird to put its head into. Make a small hole under the larger holes for a dowel that the birds can sit on. Tie twine around the top of the bottle to hang it on a tree branch. Fill the bottom of the bottle with birdseed.

Caterpillar

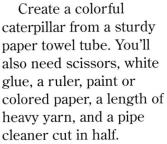

Create a colorful caterpillar from a sturdy paper towel tube. You'll also need scissors, white glue, a ruler, paint or colored paper, a length of heavy yarn, and a pipe cleaner cut in half.

Cut a section 1" to 1 1/4" wide along the length of the tube. This part can be thrown away. Cut the rest of the tube into rings about 3/4" wide. Make one ring a little wider for the head.

Paint or use colored paper to decorate the segments both inside and out. Put a face on the head segment. If you want to make eyes that stand up, cut out two small paper circles. Fold them in half, add pupils, and glue half of each circle to the head.

Lay all the segments upside down in a row about 3/4" part. Glue them to the yarn. Twist pipe cleaner antennae to the inside of the head.

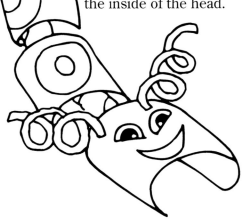

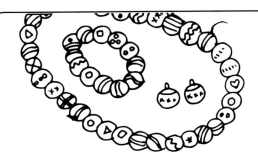

Make Your Own Jewelry From Dough

If you've been searching for a way to make gifts stamped with originality, here is the answer. Making dough jewelry is fun and foolproof. Anyone can do it; here's how.

1. Mix flour and water until the resulting dough is very stiff. Then just keep kneading it until it is completely free of lumps. A drop of perfume added to it will lend a delightful fragrance.

2. Roll the dough into a slender cylinder about a 1/2" (1.25 cm) thick; then cut beads about 1/2" (1.25 cm) long. They can be left smooth or given an attractive appearance by using the prongs of a fork to make marks in each bead.

3. When the beads are stiff but not hard, string them together by pushing a needle and heavy thread through the center of each bead, allowing about 1/2" (1.25 cm) of thread to separate each bead. Then allow them to dry thoroughly.

4. After the beads are dried and hard, paint them with watercolors, or just dip them into paint. Then coat the beads with clear nail polish.

5. Now remove the original string and re-thread them with good mercerized thread. You can make a matching bracelet and earrings (use only one bead for each earring). Clip or screw earring backs can be purchased at any craft store; just glue them to the bead back. These make great gifts for students to give to parents and grandparents.

Window Fish

Materials

- blown-out egg for each fish
- 20" (50 cm) ribbon
- Easter-egg dye
- sequins (optional)
- white felt
- white glue

Directions

1. Dip the blown-out egg carefully into desired egg dye color. Let dry.

2. Using the patterns, cut two tails and lots of scales from white felt.

3. Give your fish two sequin eyes and a mouth. Glue the tail on smaller end of egg.

4. Glue the scales on the top part of the eggshell, straight edge against the shell. One sequin may be glued to the tip of each scale if you wish.

5. Glue ribbon to the top of fish and tie ends in a bow.

Hang your fish from the window. With a little breeze blowing in from the window, your fish looks like it is alive. It makes a lovely gift for someone in the hospital.

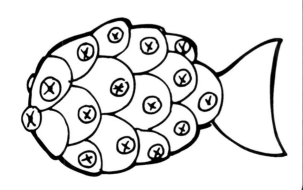

The Great Snowman Collage

Spark enthusiasm for wintertime by creating a snowman collage with the help of your class. Cut a big snowman shape out of white butcher paper. Display the snowman on a bulletin board. Ask your students to bring in pictures pertaining to winter. Create a seasonal collage by gluing these pictures on the snowman.

Make a Moonscape

Show students pictures of the moon's surface. Young students can form the valleys, hills, and craters with clay. Older students may enjoy working with papier-mâché.

Soak pieces of newspaper in a bowl of paste and cold water. Using a cardboard base, build hills and craters; then paint. Crumple sheets of soaked paper for the hills, then cover with smaller pieces. Use small pieces to form craters.

Construction-Paper Loop Art

Cut construction paper into various strips and staple the strips into loops, as in the diagrams below.

Bunny

Using one 8 1/2" × 11" (22 × 28 cm) sheet of pink construction paper, cut into one 5" × 11" (13 × 28 cm) piece (for the body) and one 3 1/2" × 11" (9 × 28 cm) piece (for the head).

Cut out two ears and two front paws from white paper. Attach the ears to the top of the head and the paws to the bottom of the head piece.

Draw on facial features with markers. Glue on a cotton ball for a tail. Staple the head and body together.

Chick

Cut two 1 1/2" strips of yellow construction paper. Cut out small orange strips for feet and a tail and attach as shown.

Cut out an orange paper beak and glue it to the head. Draw eyes with a black marker. Staple the head and body together.

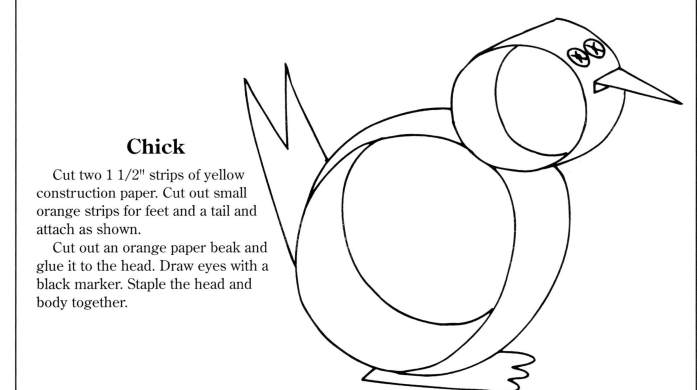

Whimsical Windsocks

The popular windsock is seen flying everywhere across the country. Making paper windsocks is an exciting activity to enrich a unit on weather, seasons, or March winds.

After a study of kinds of weather, weather facts, and weather words, pass out six butcher-paper strips cut to 21" × 3" (53 × 8 cm) to each student. Each strip should be a different color. The class can then begin making the windsock bodies. Instruct students to illustrate with as many different pictures as possible the following weather categories on the various colored strips: rain, snow, sun, clouds, storms, wind. (The four seasons could be adapted to this idea as well.) Students will enjoy enhancing their pictures with glitter and stars. Have each student glue the six strips edge-to-edge to form a rectangle.

While this dries, pass out six more colored strips cut to 16" × 1 1/2" (40 × 4 cm) for the windsock tails. Have students show how much they know about weather by writing all the weather facts and words they can think of on each tail strip. (Brainstorming together elicits a wealth of ideas.)

When each student is finished, have him or her glue the end of each tail strip to the bottom of the windsock body.

Next, have students roll the windsocks and glue the sides together to make cylinder shapes. Have them add yarn handles, and the windsocks are ready to decorate your classroom.

Your students will love "flying" home with their beautiful creations.

A Sweet May Day Basket

Materials
- one berry basket
- a few lollipops with straight sticks
- plastic foam or clay
- real or artificial flowers and greenery
- black marker
- yarn
- construction paper
- tape

Directions

On each cellophane lollipop wrapper, draw a smiling face with the marker. (Do not draw on the candy!) Tape a real or artificial flower on each lollipop like a hat. Tie a yarn bow under each lollipop face.

Fit foam (or clay) into the bottom of the berry basket. Construction-paper strips can be woven along the sides of the berry basket if you wish. Now push the lollipop sticks into the foam or clay with the "flower people" facing out. Push a few sprigs of greenery around the lollipops and add a yarn bow to the basket. Your May basket is ready to give!

Teepees

Materials
- paper sacks
- crayons
- toothpicks
- glue
- tempera paint (brown)

Directions

1. Soak the sacks in water until the seams open. Then crumple them up and squeeze out the excess water. Carefully smooth them out and let dry.

2. After the sacks have dried, cut out semicircle shapes and draw on Native American designs with crayons. Be sure to press hard! Paint over the designs with a thin coat of brown tempera paint.

3. When the paint has dried, glue toothpicks poking out of the top in the center of the straight side. Fold over the semicircle so it will form a cone and staple or glue the edges near the top. Fold over the bottom flap to give an appearance of a door or small opening.

Sunflower Tissue-Paper Art

Directions

1. Reproduce a pattern for a sunflower.

2. Have a lot of pieces of brown and yellow tissue paper cut into 2" × 2" (5 × 5 cm) squares.

3. Wrap a tissue paper square around the eraser of a pencil and dip it lightly into glue. Press the glued tip onto the pattern—brown in the center and yellow on the petals. Continue placing tissue paper around the pattern until all of the white paper is covered. Tissue paper should be placed close together.

4. A stem and background can be added to complete the project.

A School Bookmark

Go outdoors and find two small flowers and two small leaves. To add variety to the bookmark, try to find different colored flowers. Lay a heavy book on the flowers and leaves overnight to flatten them.

Using two sheets of clear adhesive paper, place the flattened flowers and leaves on one sheet's sticky side. Be sure to keep the flowers and leaves within a 2 1/2" (6 cm) wide and 5 1/2" (14 cm) long space.

Press the second sheet of adhesive paper, sticky-side down, on top of the first sheet. They should now be firmly stuck together with the leaves and flowers showing through.

Cut a 2 1/2"(6 cm) wide and 5 1/2" (14 cm) long rectangle around the flowers and leaves. If pinking shears are used, the edges of the bookmark will appear jagged.

Punch a small hole at the top of the bookmark, using either a hole punch or the pointy end of a pair of scissors.

Finally, thread a 12" (30 cm) piece of narrow ribbon through the hole. Bring the two ends together so each side is 6" (15 cm) long. Tie the two ends together, placing the knot near the hole.

Potpourri Containers

Throwaway items can often be recycled into useful, attractive objects. For example, little plastic baskets or other containers can be made into pretty potpourri containers.

Wrap a small amount of your favorite fragrant dried flower and/or herb potpourri in a small square of nylon net, and place it inside one of the little plastic baskets. Now all you need to do is decorate the exterior of the little basket. You can use bits of lace, ribbon, tiny silk flowers, or other trims to make the basket as pleasing to the eye as the potpourri is pleasing to the nose.

Fun and Easy Puppets

These puppets are easily made, and each one can be given an individual appearance. They are very versatile and can be used by very young children.

Materials

- old tennis balls (ask P.E. teachers, country clubs, or sports clubs)

- sharp carpet cutter or very sharp knife (adult use only)

- black, brown, or blue felt-tip markers

- one 1' (.30 m) square of cloth for each puppet

- yarn (hair colors)

- glue

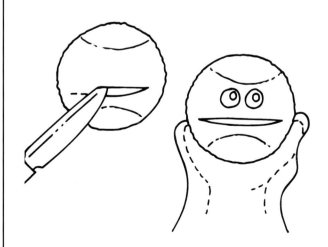

Directions

Before class, cut tennis balls as shown. By squeezing gently on the sides of the ball, the mouth will open.

Student can draw the eyes using felt-tip makers and attach hair with glue. A square piece of cloth can be draped about the hand of the puppeteer who tucks the ends of cloth into his or her hand.

How to Make a Pile of Junk

Recycling has never been more important than it is now. Landfills are filling at an alarming rate, so it is necessary for us to teach our children about the importance of recycling.

Would you like to show students how to make an interesting statement about life? How about teaching them how to make a junk-pile paperweight? This is a fun and easy project that will give you and your students hours of fun as well as serve as a great conversation piece.

Here is how you can make a "pile of junk" from various items collected around home and school.

Supplies
- pieces of waxed paper to work on
- white craft glue
- shoeboxes to store supplies in
- lid from a wide-mouthed jar

Collect your "junk" (any or all of the following)
- packing pellets
- rubber bands
- paper clips
- empty glue bottles
- empty tape rolls
- old pens/pencils
- beads from broken bracelets or necklaces
- washers and nuts
- small pieces of wood
- Mom's old costume jewelry
- twist ties from bread bags

Directions
1. Divide all "junk" into separate shoeboxes.

2. Place your jar lid on the waxed paper. This will be the base of your paperweight.

3. Start by filling the bottom of the lid first, gluing any of your "junk" to it. After the base is covered, continue to pile and glue items on so that your paper weight grows wide as well as tall. Just be careful not to make your project too tall. Remember the glue needs time to dry and the paperweight will topple if it gets too tall.

In short, any item which is no bigger than a child's hand and is safe and clean to handle may be used. Just when students think they've collected enough "junk," they will find something else to add to their "junk" piles. And when these are put on display, your students will be sure to get many comments and compliments.

Social Studies Activities

Social Studies

Tell students to select any foreign country. Ask them to imagine they had to send a greeting card to someone in that country wishing them a happy May Day or any other holiday. What type of picture should be on the front of the card? What greetings should be included? Have students fold large sheets of art paper to make and decorate cards. When the cards are complete, use a large world map to locate countries for which the cards have been created.

Loads of Logs

Cut quite a few "Lincoln Logs" from brown posterboard or cardboard. Print a question relating to Abraham Lincoln on each of them for the students to answer. (It might be a good idea to have some books on Abraham Lincoln readily available for students to use in the classroom.) Some examples of questions are given below, but feel free to make up many more of your own in order to adapt them more specifically to the students. When all the questions are answered, the class could get together and write a research paper about the life of Abraham Lincoln.

Store the logs in a can covered with black sticky paper and with a round piece of black posterboard or cardboard glued to the bottom of the can to resemble a hat worn by Lincoln.

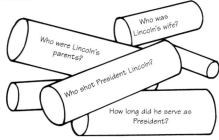

Geography Fun

For a real test of your students' resourcefulness, have them go on a Seasonal Geography Hunt. The object is to find a winter-related city, mountain, lake, river, landmark, and so on, in every state. It can even be the state itself, such as Washington (February). Other winter examples include: Lincoln, Nebraska; Snowmass Mountain in Colorado; or Lake Placid, New York (site of the 1980 Winter Olympics). Provide maps, almanacs, encyclopedias—anything that can be used as reference. This could even be turned into a contest with the student having the most answers at the end of the designated time limit being the winner.

Capital Match

Materials

- shoebox
- cards
- glue
- old U.S. puzzle
- old U.S. map
- gummed stars
- wooden craft sticks
- small juice can
- colored sticky paper

Preparations

1. Glue the states from an old U.S. puzzle on the cards. Put the names of the state capitals on the backs.
2. Color the tips of wooden sticks either red, white, or blue.
3. Cover a juice can with colored sticky paper.
4. Make a card that says, Red—1 card, White—2 cards, Blue—3 cards.
5. Provide gummed stars for awards. Store everything in a shoebox that has been covered with states cut from old maps.

Directions

1. Take out the can and sticks. Put the colored ends of the sticks into the bottom of the can.
2. Take out the color-code card but leave the state cards in the shoebox. Make sure that they are answer side down.
3. Player 1 draws a stick from the can. If he draws a red stick, he gets to draw one state card from the box. If he correctly names the capital, he keeps the card and puts the stick back into the can. If he does not answer correctly, he puts the state card back into the box.
4. Player 2 then goes. The winner is the one with the most state cards at the end of the game.

Going on Vacation!

Separate the class into small groups. Give each group a road map with which to work. The assignment is to plan an imaginary vacation for your group. Have each group choose a destination. Use the following questions to get the class started. Expand the list yourself, or let students come up with more questions.

1. What is the closest way to get to your destination? Write down the route numbers that you must follow.

2. What is the best alternative route (another way to get there)?

3. What means of transportation will you use to get to your destination? (plane, train, boat, car)

4. What specific things might you see along the way? (forests, campgrounds, monuments, and so on)

5. How many county lines will you cross over? What counties will you go through?

6. Will you have to cross any state lines? Which ones?

7. Will you stop and rest? Where? For how long?

8. Will you cross any rivers or lakes? Name them.

9. What do you plan to do on your vacation?

10. Whom are you planning to take with you?

11. For this time of year, what kinds of clothes will you pack? Will the weather be the same as it is here?

12. What supplies will you need to take with you?

Learning About the Past

It's sometimes hard for students to relate to people like George Washington or Abraham Lincoln since they lived so long ago. This project will help to bring these people and the times in which they lived into focus.

Write a Newspaper

Write (and make photocopies for other classes) your own "News of the Times." Write it as if everything were happening today. Include famous people in the news, such as "Betsy Ross Starts Sewing Nation's First Flag" or "Lincoln Declares Slavery at an End."

With lots of research, each item will come alive and become a fun and interesting way to review history. Assign half of the class to the Washington paper and half to the Lincoln paper.

Interviews With Washington and Lincoln

Pick two students to portray Washington and Lincoln, and others to be important people connected with their lives (such as Martha Washington and Mary Todd Lincoln).

Stress that everyone must be adequately prepared, since you'll expect the "audience" to be asking important questions that the speakers should be prepared to answer.

Have your Mr. Washington wear a three-sided hat and Mr. Lincoln wear a black stovepipe hat and beard.

Sailing on the *Niña, Pinta,* and *Santa Maria*

Columbus used three ships—the *Niña,* the *Pinta,* and the *Santa Maria*—to explore a new world.

Divide students into groups of three. Show pictures of ships similar to those of this period. Supply students with large cardboard boxes, white fabric or durable paper, a dowel rod for the mast, tape, and art supplies. Have students design their own ships. After the ships are complete, invite another class to view your students' creative talents. Later, place the ships in a reading center for the month of October.

An Interview With Columbus

During your study of this famous explorer, plan an interview with your subject. Guide students to research information about the late 1400s, the life of Columbus, and other historical facts. You may want to assign one student to take the part of Columbus and dress in a costume of this period. Class members may use their questions as a way of gathering information or as a review of the unit.

Journal of My Voyage With Columbus

The world was changed by Columbus and others like him. In proving that the world was round instead of flat, he opened the way for other explorers. Ask students to pretend they are sailors who Columbus convinced to accompany him in search of the New World. Have them keep a journal of their "journey."

Start the first entry on August 3, 1492, and end with October 12, 1492. Suggest students make at least one notation for each week during this time span.

Post these words or phrases to stimulate creative thoughts:

breezes	tide	water
sky	birds	sea monsters
mistake	sour food	stale water
sickness	fear	doubt
hunger	storms	the unknown
branch	land	beach
Native Americans		

Make Your Own Mountain

This is a fun hands-on geography project. With clay, form a mountain. Add trees made from pipe cleaners and flowers made from cardboard. Place the mountain on a wooden surface and make it large enough to carve in paths and rivers. Paint the grassy areas green and brown, and the top white with snow.

United Nations Feast

With the help of parents, prepare a United Nations feast with foods from around the world. Below are some suggested foods your class might try.

Rice (a staple in Asia)
Yams or Sweet Potatoes (Africa)
Bean Cakes (Asia)
Cornmeal Cakes (Central and South America)
Yogurt (Asia)
Pasta (Southern Europe)
Flat Pancakes (Russia)
Cheese (worldwide)

Send invitations for the United Nations celebrations to the principal, school secretary, lunchroom aides, and other school personnel.

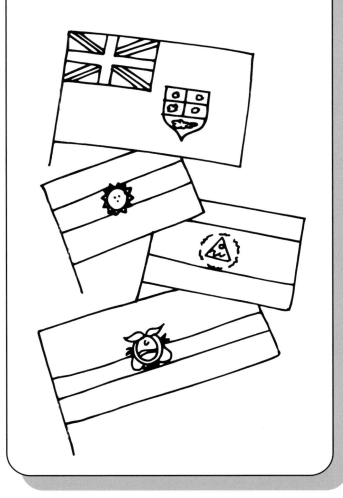

United Nations Bulletin Board

Enlarge an outline map of the world. Attach a United Nations label or small flag to as many member nations as you can fit on the map. Following are some of the 185 U.N. members: Argentina, Australia, Belgium, Bolivia, Brazil, Canada, Dominican Republic, Ecuador, Egypt, El Salvador, Ethiopia, France, Greece, Guatemala, Honduras, India, Lebanon, Luxembourg, Mexico, Netherlands, New Zealand, Nicaragua, Norway, Paraguay, United Kingdom, and United States of America.

The hope of the United Nations is that through peaceful discussions, violent conflicts can be avoided. With your students, talk about ways in which they could help keep peace within their class, school, and community. From that discussion, help each student record his or her wish for peace. Record these wishes on strips of blue paper, 2" × 8" (5 × 20 cm) long. Make a paper chain out of the wishes, with every other link being made from plain blue paper. For your bulletin board, form the chain into a circle with the wishes toward the outside, and staple together, attaching the links to the previous round. A 50-link chain will make a 25" to 28" (64 to 71 cm) circle. Over the blue circle, add a white cutout of the continents. Using the olive leaf pattern, cut out 4 branches and 16 leaves from white paper. Make a vine along the side similar to the one that appears on the United Nations flag. Over the top, write the caption *Peace for Our World Family*.

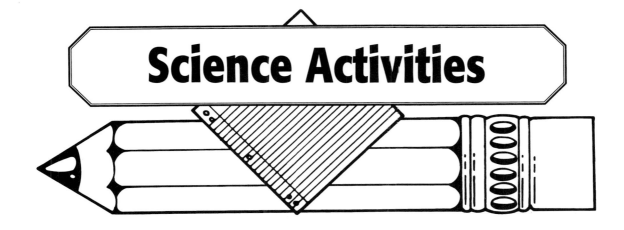

Science Activities

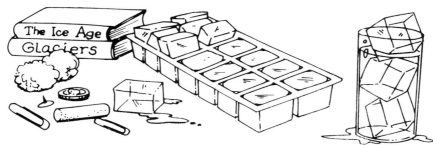

Fun With Ice Cubes and Snowballs

- Let students try all sorts of ways to get an ice cube to melt. No hot water allowed! Try radiators, fans, crushing, and so on. Each student will think of plenty of ways to make his or her ice cube melt the fastest.

- Then have a contest to determine who can keep an ice cube frozen the longest. No refrigerators or freezers allowed! Supply newspapers, sandwich bags, foil, boxes, cotton, and so on. Set a time limit, possibly overnight, to see whose cube remains the largest.

- Try putting different things on an ice cube: a penny, a washer, thumbtacks, wood, chalk, a ring, salt, paper, a paper clip.

- Float ice cubes in water, oil, salt water, or alcohol. What happens? Does an ice cube melt faster than a snowball? Color some ice cubes yellow, some red, some blue. Serve them in pairs in lemonade. What happens? This is a nice thing to do at a party during the winter season.

- Older students may study the Ice Age. Find out what a glacier is. How was it formed? Where are glaciers found today?

- Provide containers in a variety of sizes and shapes in which you can freeze water. Use these containers to make funny-shaped ice cubes. Which cubes melt the fastest? Time the melting process.

- Bring a snowball in from outside. Put it in a dish. Have students write down what time it is and how long they think it will take the snowball to melt. Each student then figures how many minutes "off" he or she was.

- Bring some snow into the classroom. Put it in several dishes of different sizes. Cover some dishes with paper and others with leaves. Sand, salt, rocks, cloth, and soil can also be used. Which dish of snow melts the fastest? Why?

Experimenting With Prisms

Problem—How can a liquid act as a prism?

Materials
- a light source (flashlight, film projector)
- bowl/small pan
- pocket mirror

Procedure

Discuss with students the colors of the rainbow and the spectrum formed when light passes through a prism. Explain that if water takes a triangular shape, it may act as a prism and break light into its component colors.

Next, give each group a pan or bowl of water, a light source, and a mirror (preferably about 2" × 3" [5 × 8 cm]). Instruct students to attempt to arrange the materials so that a spectrum is formed. Darken the room so that if spectra are reflected on the wall or ceiling, they will be seen more easily.

If no students discover the right solution, instruct them as follows: Place the mirror in the pan or bowl of water so that one end rests on the edge and the other is on the bottom. Be sure not to proceed until the water has settled because rippling water will not work. When a mirror is angled through the water in this way, a triangular area of water is created. Now, shine the light source at about a 45° angle toward the mirror. Try various angles. A spectrum will be reflected by the mirror on the wall or ceiling. Have some students try this using glycerine or mineral oil as liquids in place of water.

This experiment shows how water may act as a prism and also provides students with an opportunity to manipulate materials and make observations.

Sponge Garden

The following idea can be used in conjunction with science units dealing with plants and seeds. It's fun for students to see how different seeds look as they grow.

Soak a sponge and put it in a dish of water. Sprinkle seeds over the top of the sponge. Try different kinds of seeds that might be left over from planting a garden. Grass seed and birdseed also work well.

Keep water in the dish so the sponge doesn't dry out. When leaves appear, you'll know that the food stored in the seeds is used up. Add liquid plant food to the water to keep your plants healthy.

Watch your sponge garden. You'll be surprised at how tall it grows!

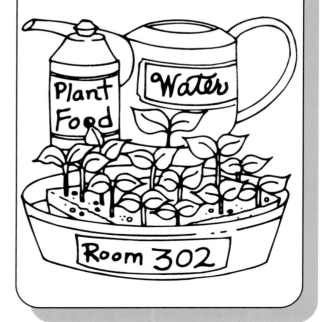

Weather Art

This is a fun way to include art in your daily weather forecasts. Select one student to be the artist who will serve for a week at a time. Portion a part of your bulletin board for weather forecasts. The student or students responsible for posting the weather report for the day places their notice on the bulletin board. The artist for the week reads the report and sketches a scene to illustrate the prediction: a rainy scene on a rainy day, a sunshiny scene on a sunshiny day, a snowy scene when it snows, and so on. The scene is placed under or beside the forecast on the bulletin board. Change artists and weather reporters after they have served for a week to allow others to participate. If space allows, you may leave the daily forecasts and illustrations up for the entire week so that all students will have sufficient time to read and reread the bulletins and enjoy the art.

Through this activity, students become more proficient in reading weather words. They begin to understand the use of degrees; wind velocity and direction; what highs and lows are; cold fronts; symbols used by weather forecasters for rain, snow, air flow, and so on. They get to know the use of the word *percent,* and concepts such as *light and variable.*

Newspaper weather reports will probably be used more by students than the TV reports as it is easier to clip the newspaper bulletin than it is to jot down what the TV reporter says. However, both will be used from time to time.

Shadow Clock

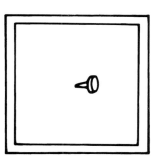

Explain to students that they can use shadows to help tell time.

Tape a sheet of white paper to a piece of heavy cardboard. Stick a nail through the center of the paper and cardboard leaving most of the nail showing.

Have students go outside early on a sunny day and find a flat spot to lay the cardboard. Use a few small rocks to hold the cardboard in place.

Start marking the shadow of the nail on the paper with a pencil. Every hour or so, mark where the shadow is on the paper. Be sure to write the time above the mark.

The next day, have students check their shadow clocks to see if they tell the right time.

Discuss whether or not the clocks would tell the right time if someone moved the cardboard. Do students think the clocks will be right on time a week later? A month later? All year long?

Invite ROY G. BIV to Your Classroom

Why not invite Roy G. Biv to your classroom for a science and art lesson? His initial appearance might be via a prism or a simple chandelier crystal catching the sunlight through the window. Students can make observations about the rainbow patterns made by the prism.

Have each student take out his or her crayons and locate red, orange, yellow, green, blue, indigo, and violet. On a large sheet of butcher paper, each student or group can design the following character: Mr. Roy G. Biv has a red ball on his orange hat and a yellow face with a green beard. He has a blue shirt and mittens, indigo pants, and violet boots.

Younger children may enjoy coloring an outline drawing of Mr. Biv.

Have students research why the colors of the rainbow are always in a particular order and what causes a rainbow, a double rainbow, and so on. Students can write poems, myths, or legends about rainbows and their origins.

Students can make small line drawings of themselves or Mr. Biv and then lightly write their names in cursive so that each figure is holding the name, like a jump rope or a lasso. Using seven strands of bright yarn, glue them on in the correct rainbow order so that the name is seven strands wide.

Poor Richard

Introduce the almanac to the class. Explain how many people use the phases of the moon to determine when to plant crops. Provide shapes of the moon's phases to attach to the classroom calendar each day.

Home Sweet Moon

It is the year 2050. Living space on Earth has become scarce. Plans are made to colonize the moon. What elements would be necessary for human survival on the moon? Describe the facility you would build for the colonists.

Dancing Germs

Find pictures of bacteria and viruses in encyclopedias. Provide students with a variety of materials for creating imaginary germs. These might include: yarn, toilet tissue cores, chenille stems, and 1 1/4" (3 cm) and 1/4" (.6 cm) gummed circles. You will also need large and medium sewing needles, and black thread. Some ideas are shown here. Your students will probably have many more.

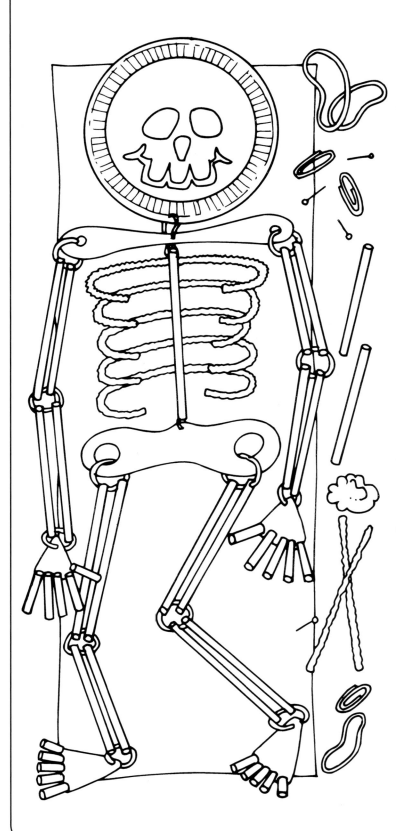

The First Annual Awesome Skeleton-Building Contest

The First Annual Awesome Skeleton Building Contest can be used to top off a unit on the skeletal system. Provide each student with the following materials:

- 1 paper plate
- 1 blob of white clay
- 10 rubber bands
- 14 plastic straws
- 1 piece of white paper
- 4 paper clips
- 14 pipe cleaners
- 10 straight pins

Have scissors, tape, and glue available to everyone. The time limit is one hour.

Objective: Build a model human skeleton, standing or hanging.

Rules: Use only the materials you have. You do not have to use all the materials, but leftovers must be put away in their original containers.

Awards: Skeleton stickers on note cards with the following captions can be presented:

> First One Done
>
> Tallest
>
> Shortest
>
> Most Realistic
>
> Sturdiest Rib Cage
>
> You choose criteria

What a variety of skeletons can be created! The hour passes quickly with not a sound coming from the young scientists. Completed skeletons can be displayed against a black paper background.

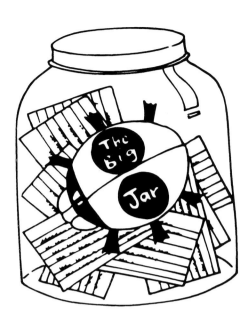

The Bug Jar Trivia Game

Send your students on an insect trivia hunt to help make a class trivia game. Students may use encyclopedias and other reference books to research their information.

Divide your class into small teams and ask each team to write questions (with answers) on 3" × 5" (8 × 13 cm) cards on their assigned subject. Some suggested categories are: ants, butterflies, bees, crickets, grasshoppers, flies, and beetles. Have a brainstorming session with your class to add more to the list.

Put the completed trivia question cards in a large glass jar labeled **The Bug Jar** and play a round or two during those extra minutes of the day!

To further extend this activity, teachers may want to have each trivia team write a mini report on its assigned insect to be presented to the class. Some suggestions are: making poster reports (with pictures and facts), creating a television game show or news program that features their insect facts, and an imaginary interview with an entomologist.

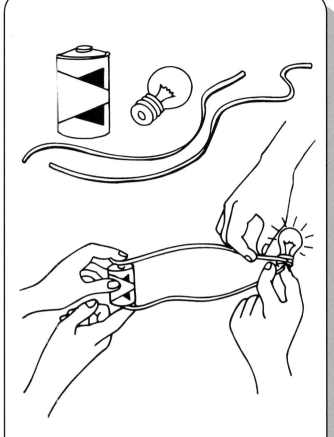

Make a Simple Flashlight

Materials
- 1 flashlight battery cell (size C or D)
- 1 flashlight bulb for a 1- or 2-cell flashlight
- 2 copper wires (14 to 20 gauge)

Student Instructions

With a partner, have your helper hold the cell in his or her hands and press one end of each wire against *each* terminal of the cell (bottom and center terminals). Hold the bulb down on a wooden tabletop and place the loose end of *one* wire against the metal side of the bulb.

Place the loose end of the *other* wire on the center connection of the bulb bottom. The bulb should light.

Note: A serviceable light can be made by soldering the connections at battery and bulb and inserting a small switch in one of the wires.

Seek and Find— Then Classify

Ask your class to collect a variety of rocks, looking for different colors, sizes, shapes, and textures. If you do not live in an area where a field trip is convenient, it works just as well to use a rock collection from a local library or your school's library.

Once you have your rocks, you are set to go! Divide the class into groups of three or four. Ask students to make separate piles of their rocks according to color, size, shape, texture, and luster. Encourage them to think up their own ideas for other categories.

To enhance math skills, chart results by listing the number of rocks that fit into each category.

Nests, Insects, Rocks, and Shells

Spark your students' enthusiasm for science by creating your own classroom science museum. You can transform an area with empty shelves into one of the most popular spots at school! Here's how to create your museum.

1. Have a brainstorming session with your class and talk about your plans to have a museum.

2. Have students vote on a name for your museum. With students' help, decide on the categories of items you would like to display in your museum. Some suggestions are: shells, rocks, nests, insects, seeds, leaves and bark, ocean creatures (dried starfish, seahorses), and so on.

3. Make bright, laminated signs to label each shelf with its category. Line your shelves with colorful construction paper. You may want to set up a microscope mini center nearby to enable students to take a closer look at some of the museum items, such as leaves and seeds.

4. When the museum is ready, encourage students to bring in items to share with the class. Have them label each item with their name for easy identification.

The Straw Plunger

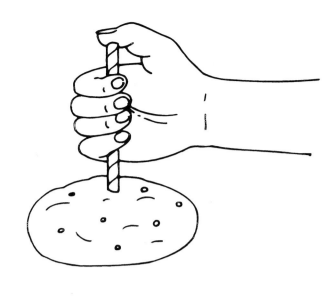

1. **Materials:** one firm raw potato and one plastic drinking straw per person

2. **Procedure:** Cover one end of the straw with your thumb. Plunge the straw straight down into the potato. You may need to try several times to get the right angle and force.

3. Carefully remove the straw and see what, if anything, is in the straw. Why and how did this work?

Electrically Charged Straws

1. **Materials:** a small hill of salt and pepper and one drinking straw per person

2. **Procedure:** Rub a straw against dry hair or wool clothing. Will the straw stick to anything? What? If it can stick, why is it possible?

3. Now rub the straw again and hold it over the hill of salt and pepper. What happens? Was the salt and pepper attracted to the straw? Why or why not?

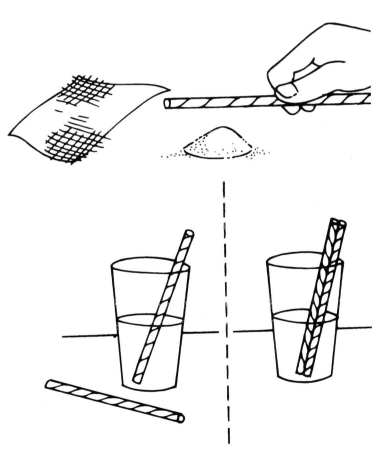

The Straw Elevator

1. **Materials:** two drinking straws per person; a colored beverage; and one clear glass per person, partially filled with the colored drink

2. **Procedure:** Place one straw in a glass of the colored beverage. Sip on the straw. Is it easy to drink? How does it work?

3. Place the second straw in the glass of drink and sip again. Will you get more to drink by using two straws rather than one? Why?

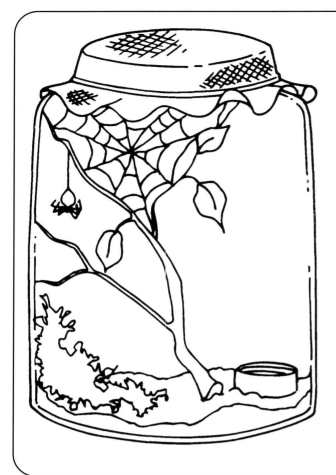

A Spider Is Watching

Instead of the usual classroom observation of a spider, reverse the situation: invite a spider to observe the classroom.

For a spider's-eye view of your world, you will need a gallon-sized glass jar. Add two cups of sand or soil and a bit of moss. A couple of twigs with leaves attached will support a web, plus provide a nook for hiding. Fill a bottle cap with water for thirsty inhabitants. Secure a piece of cheesecloth or netting over the top with a rubber band. Now, your habitat is ready for its first occupant. Locate a garden spider or another web-builder. With a stick, carefully place the spider in a small container. Transfer to the terrarium. Encourage students to observe and record data, using these questions:

1. What type of web is the spider building?
2. What are its favorite insects? (Place a fly, grasshopper, or others inside.)
3. When is the spider most active?

Return the spider to the outside in a few days and replace with another species. Compare the two spiders.

Salt and Ice

How does salt affect water's ability to freeze?

Materials
- 1 ice-cube tray
- water
- measuring spoons
- tablespoon
- table salt

Procedure

1. Fill each of the spaces in the ice-cube tray with 1 tablespoon (15 ml) of water.
2. Leave plain water in two of the spaces.
3. Add 1/8 teaspoon (.625 ml) salt to each of the next two spaces.
4. Add 1/4 teaspoon (1.25 ml) salt to the next two spaces.
5. Continue adding an extra 1/8 teaspoon (.625 ml) salt every two spaces until all the spaces are filled.
6. Put the tray in the freezer.
7. After about two hours, check the ice-cube tray. What observations can students make? What is their conclusion about how salt affects the freezing of water?

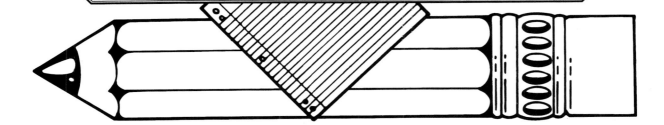

Seasonal Activities

Hands-on Patriotism

 Here is a project that can involve everyone in the school: students, teachers, custodians, the principal, cafeteria workers, and even bus drivers. Creating the American flag from paper hands can be a fun activity for February—the birth month of two great presidents. Just have each person trace his or her hands and cut them out. A little planning will determine who should be red, white, or blue. Then have one student from each class outline his or her body, color it, and cut it out. Don't forget to include a couple of adults. These figures can be placed beneath the flag to represent those who worked on the project. Finally, find a large space near the entrance of the school or in the gym or cafeteria to tape up the flag. If the hands are glued on large strips of paper before being placed on the wall, the flag could be used for several years.

Paper Plate Presidents

 Have each student make the face of a president on a paper plate, using the outer edge as the head. Make hair of yarn or cotton (wigs). Have students look at pictures of the presidents as they make their paper-plate presidents. Each student can make the president of his or her choice.

Uses

- Put the presidents up around the room in sequential order, with the dates of the presidencies below each.
- Put the presidents on tongue depressors and make puppets out of them.
- Have a puppet that is a reporter. Have the reporter interview the presidents to find out critical information about them, their presidencies, and the times in which they lived.

Glossy Eggs

 Cut out large egg shapes from heavy white paper (something similar to watercolor paper). Open a can of condensed milk and pour into several containers. Add drops of food coloring to each to make lovely pastel paints. Using cotton swabs, paint Easter designs all over the paper eggs. Lay these flat to dry; they will take a couple of days to dry thoroughly. The smooth, glossy surface is surely worth the wait.

The Real Meaning of *Love*

Valentine's Day is a fun holiday with thoughts of sweethearts and valentines filling our heads. Since love is the focus of the day, let students show love to someone in a special way.

1. Have each student bring in an old toy. Then have a Fix-Up-and-Repair Day. With a little cleaning, painting, and gluing, the toys will soon look like new. Donate these "new" toys to a children's hospital or foster care center.

2. Organize a We Can Help Make a Difference food drive involving the whole school. Place boxes around the building and encourage everyone to contribute a can of food. After the boxes are filled, deliver them to a local food bank.

3. Call your local humane society and arrange for a speaker to talk about unwanted and abused animals and what students can do to help these animals. Have students bring cans of pet food to be given to abused and unwanted animals at the animal shelter.

A Jar of Valentines

How about letting your students make no-calorie valentine candy "jars" to take home to friends and relatives? The jars of hearts can also be used as valentine cards.

The candy jars and valentines can be made from construction paper (any size you wish). Have each student fold a piece of white paper in half lengthwise and then draw half the jar on one side of the paper. Then cut out the jar and unfold it. Hearts can be cut out of red and pink construction paper. Each student can write personalized messages on the hearts for whomever is to receive the jar. Glue the completed hearts to the candy jar.

Variation

Cut two jars exactly the same size from waxed paper. Place the valentines on the waxy side of one of the jars and place the other waxed paper jar waxed-side down on top of the valentines. An adult or older student should then iron the jars together so that the two pieces of waxed paper stick together with the valentines between them.

Autumn Leaves

Each student draws a funny face on yellow, red, and orange paper leaves. The leaves are all put into a paper bag. Two teams play the game, the September Team and the October Team. The red leaves score 10 points; the yellow leaves score 4 points; the orange leaves score no points.

One student at a time, on alternating teams, takes one leaf from the bag and holds on to it. The teams continue to take turns until all the leaves have been taken from the bag. Then add up the scores for the leaves the students hold. The highest team score wins. The winning team cuts out a brown paper tree and tapes it to the wall. The top of the tree has a blank area for students to glue on their leaves. When the funny face leaves are glued in place, the personality tree becomes a wall decoration for everyone to enjoy.

Christmas Card Holder

Materials
- cereal box
- construction paper
- cotton balls
- paper stars
- glue

Directions
1. Cut off the top of a cereal box so the front and back are about 6" (15 cm) high and the sides are about 4" (10 cm) high.

2. Cover the box with dark blue or black construction paper. Cut a circle from pink construction paper for a Santa face. Also cut out small circles for Santa's eyes, nose, and mouth and glue on the face in the proper places. From red construction paper, make a Santa hat and glue the hat on Santa's head.

3. Glue Santa's head onto the box. Use cotton balls to make Santa's beard and trim his hat. Glue the paper stars to the dark paper background. When Christmas cards start to arrive, they can be kept in this festive holder.

Thanksgiving Cookbook

Have your class create a Thanksgiving cookbook. Each student writes one recipe. The fun part of this project is that students make up their own recipes. (You may have to write or help younger children with their recipes.) It's much easier to have students write on 8" × 5" (20 × 13 cm) recipe cards. Students can illustrate their cards if they have enough space and then display them on your Thanksgiving Feast bulletin board.

Hints

* Be sure to explain what a recipe card should contain.

* Let students choose their favorite kinds of foods for their recipes. Talk about a balanced diet, good nutrition, and so on.

* Run off copies of the recipes and make a cookbook to send home to parents. They will enjoy it!

Decorative Thanksgiving Plate

Cut out a circle from orange posterboard and cover it with a paper doily. Trim the posterboard circle to match the doily. Glue a soft foam picnic plate to the center. Next, cut a circle of brown construction paper the same size as the picnic plate and glue it to the bottom of the plate. Leave edges of the construction paper unglued and fold up to form a ruffle. Glue ribbon along the inside edge of the ruffle as shown in the picture. Add pumpkins and leaves cut from construction paper. Write *We Give Thanks* on the plate and add gold glitter for extra sparkle.

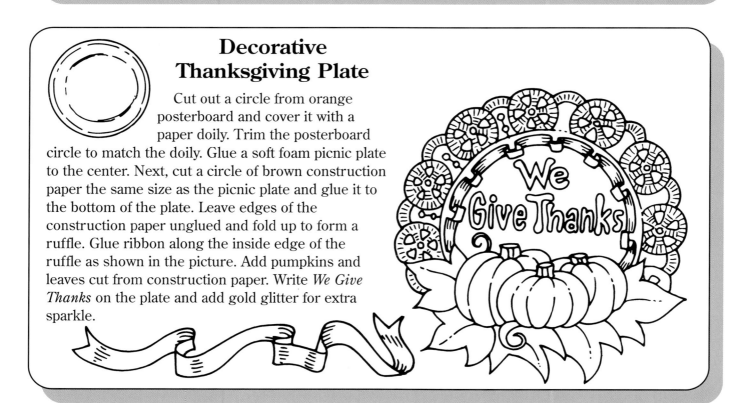

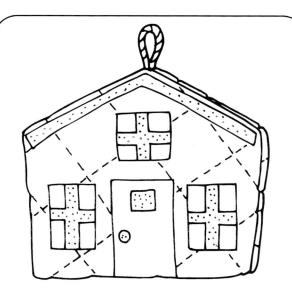

Christmas Tree House Ornaments

Cut out a cardboard pattern of a house. Trace the pattern of the house onto another piece of cardboard. Glue quilted cotton cloth cut from the same pattern onto both sides of your cardboard house. Cut out colorful felt windows and doors to glue onto both sides. Using white glue, cut out and glue felt strips along the edges of the roof on each side. Staple a yarn loop to the top of the house to hang on your tree.

A Christmas Tree Game

The boys compete against the girls in this game. Each student has a piece of paper to be decorated like a package tied with a ribbon. The student's name is printed on the front. On the opposite side of the package, draw a picture of a toy. Show each package and its toy to students and name its owner. Pin all of the packages onto the wall tree. Now boys compete against the girls, with alternate turns. They try to guess which toy is on the back of each package. Tell only the name on the package. Keep score to see if the boys or girls win.

Your Own Small Christmas Tree

Materials
- large thread spool
- small evergreen branch
- bits of ribbon, paper, or buttons for trim

Directions
Decorate the thread spool with bits of red and green ribbon, rickrack, or Christmas wrapping paper. Push an evergreen branch into the hole of the spool for the small tree. Decorate the tree with tiny paper chains, ribbons, bows, paper stars, buttons, or other small trim.

Winter Picnic

Tired of those long, indoor lunch hours due to subzero weather or storms? Try a winter picnic! Clear the center of the room and eat lunches there. For "extras," make Eskimo sandwiches, serve an ice-cream treat, bake white cupcakes covered with coconut, or serve real "snow cones" with syrup poured over them. Just eating lunch in the room is a big thrill.

How about asking each family to fix the student's lunch with all snowy white food? White bread, milk, cauliflower, white cupcakes, popcorn—see how imaginative a family can be.

Winter Scavenger Hunt

Learn more about winter and cold weather by planning an outdoor scavenger hunt with your class. Divide the class into pairs and give each pair a plastic bag. Set a time limit and boundary lines on the school property. Challenge students to find one item in each category.

- a bird feather
- something that is combustible
- material that will not burn
- evergreen (small piece)
- item that will decay
- item that will not decay
- something birds eat in winter
- an item animals may eat in winter
- dried twig
- a cocoon
- a dried leaf

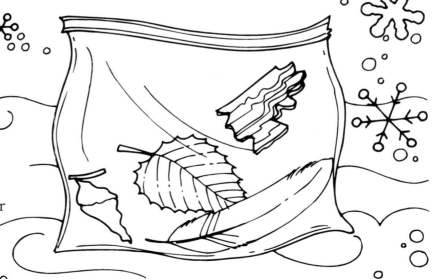

Index